WHAT DO I DO NOW

THE HONEST GUIDE TO WALKING IN YOUR PURPOSE

ANDRAE SMITH SR.

WHAT

The Honest Guide To

DO I DO

Walking In Your Purpose

NOW

ANDRAE SMITH SR.

Editing: Andrae D. Smith Jr.

Cover Design: Emily's World Of Design

To my family,
My children, Andrae, Cherelle, Londyn, & Laila
My mother, Sylvia (R.I.H)

CONTENTS

Introduction   ix

1. "I'm Lost"   1
2. My Story   6
3. The Journey   13
4. What is Purpose   19
5. Gifts, Power, & Presence   28
6. The Impact You Leave   37
7. Learning to Hear God   44
8. Your Gift Will Make Room for You   54
9. Using Your Gift Confidently   64
10. Dealing With Distractions   69
11. Making Mistakes   76
12. When God Puts His Finger On You   82
13. Forgiveness   89
14. Jealousy is the Enemy of Purpose   95
15. Humility & Responsibility   103
16. You are More Than Your Calling   108
17. Looking Ahead   115

Acknowledgements   121
About the Author   123
Thank You   125

INTRODUCTION

When most people hear my name, I'm sure the first thing that comes to mind is music. I've been known for most of my life as a talented musician, for my gift on the organ and the piano. People recognize my sound and how I use music to touch their hearts. The words "Andrae" and "book" are two that most people would never put together unless you're talking about my son, who's had a mind for writing books since he was just a child.

I remember listening to him tell me about the stories he was working on and thinking, "How can he imagine so much depth?" He had thought of nearly every detail, from the names and origins of the characters to the lineage, relationships, and symbolism that each imaginary person had. What I saw then was an anointing, and it was only a matter of time before he would share his gift with the world.

I never thought that this anointing would have a purpose for me too. My son grew up to be a writer and editor, and when I mentioned to him that I'd like to write a book someday, he sat me down at my kitchen table (imagine that, my son at twenty-six telling me at forty-four to have a seat at my table) and asked me why not now. Why didn't I start writing now? "Writing a book is easier than you think," he told me.

To make a long story short, he helped me figure it out, piece by piece. It was like building a model house with an architect as a partner. What I thought would be me just telling my story eventually became an opportunity to serve a higher good—to help people who may have a similar story or experience to mine find their paths. Just like that, purpose was injected into my book, literally and figuratively.

That is what this book is about. Purpose is something that we think we have to find, but in reality, it is something that is already there from the moment we are conceived. There is a purpose and a calling that we don't always recognize—it may show up as a talent or gift when we're young and only become apparent at the moment it is most needed, perhaps years later.

Writing this book has been a transformative experience for me as God prompts and nudges me to take the next steps in his plan for my life. I only ever saw myself behind the keys, but through writing and sharing my testimonies, I've begun to minister in new ways, which shows me that God's not done with me yet. In fact, he's just getting started.

I also want to mention that I've written this book as it came to me. I am a Christian, and this is my testimony. But that doesn't mean you have to be on the exact same path to understand this message. No matter who you are, what path you've taken so far, and where you think you are going, if you've felt lost, uncertain, or like you're ready for more, there is something in this book for you too.

As you read this book, I encourage you not to think of it as a definitive roadmap to uncovering objective purpose or what some people may call destiny, but rather a book meant to offer guidance as you embark on your own journey. Like a father imparting wisdom to a child, I hope that I can give you something to carry with you as you go.

It's my prayer for you, now, that the stories I share, which have been chosen with the intention of guiding you to your own path, serve their highest purpose in your life. It is my prayer that, by the end of this book, you feel equipped and empowered to uncover your path to purpose. Wherever you are, remember, God's just getting started.

"For I know the plans I have for you," declares the LORD, *"plans to prosper you and not to harm you, plans to give you hope and a future."*

— JEREMIAH 29:11 (*THE HOLY BIBLE* NIV)

"I'M LOST"

I remember the knot wound tight in the pit of my stomach as I approached the counter with my paperwork. It was my third attempt, and the San Bernardino County courthouse clerk had already marked up the pages with her pen twice. I couldn't tell who was getting more frustrated, her or me. I was one of the last people in that office, and it was almost time for them to close, but I was determined.

As an eighteen-year-old boy, on the precipice of manhood, I had already become a father of two beautiful children. I had also gone through my first divorce, and my ex-wife had applied for full custody. I realize, now, that I didn't know the first thing about raising two kids, but I knew that I wanted to be there for them. It was important to me that my children knew their father loved them and wanted to be there. After almost a year of court dates and failed mediations, I was almost at my limit. Almost.

On this day, I had driven to the courthouse at 7:00 am, waited in lines for hours, and failed the paperwork twice trying to figure it out alone with my sixth-grade education, all to make sure I had my shot. I arrived at the desk and handed my documents to the woman on the other side. Rolling her eyes, she smacked the papers back in front of me.

"You don't have this right," she said, "I don't know what you're even here for. You need to go get some help."

Rude as she was, I did need help. Unfortunately, there was none. I was separated from my family. The men who were around me—roommates and pastors I played the organ for and called myself looking up to—were telling me to give up. They said that my kids would remember me when they were older and that I should focus on my career. Now I realize that some of these men had a different purpose for me than what I knew I should have been doing, which I'll talk about in a later chapter. At this moment, though, it was the only counsel I had, and I was so worn out, so defeated. How was I supposed to keep fighting a losing battle? That was the final straw for me.

It's been twenty-five years since this day, and I am proud to say that I have a presence in my children's lives. It has taken a lot of learning, apologies, and effort to make up for that lost time, but we have found a way to reunite in something that looks like family. But that's not why I'm telling this story. I'm sharing it because this is a moment in my life when I felt true loss, true doubt, and what some would call despair. I had to throw my hands up and find my way again after what I thought was my purpose (my family) was lost to me.

Maybe you've felt this way at some point in your life—tired, confused, defeated, desperate for an answer about what to do next. If you have, then perhaps you can relate to this story. Perhaps you have one just like it, where you've fought for something, given your all, dedicated time and tears toward a goal or vision only to meet wall after wall or obstacle after obstacle until all you can do is lie on your back and ask, "What do I do now?"

Sometimes in life, you will fall into these valleys. If you're like me, you may even dive into a few head-first. While you're down there, it can be easy to feel like your life has stalled or like you're stuck in the slow lane, watching others race by toward a happiness you can barely imagine from where you are. You may even feel like you're in a pressure cooker, and it's getting hotter and hotter. You need a way out before you burn up and die.

Maybe this isn't your experience. Maybe your life has been more like my oldest children's. They both graduated high school top of their class and have found their own ways into college and careers and families. My daughter, the model, the scientist, bounced between a few different jobs looking for something that lived up to her financial needs and standards as an educated woman. My son, the writer, had spent years building a promising management career in a prominent retail chain.

They followed the "proper" course and were reaping the rewards of making the "right" choices. From the surface, you would never know that they were struggling at all. In reality, both of them would soon have their own "crisis moment," where they realized that they were unhappy with the lives they had been given. They both found themselves aching for something more enriching.

What do you do when what you have isn't enough to fill your cup? How do you move forward when all of the options before you feel just as empty and uninspired as where you been? It's in these moments when you may be thinking, "There has got to be more than this. I've got to be meant for than this."

Whether you're facing a life-altering struggle, or you've come to a crossroads in your life and find yourself longing for meaning, you are ready. You're being called out of your current situation and pushed toward the very thing you're seeking. Some call it "meaning" or "destiny." For this book, I'm going to call the thing that's nagging at you—that's making you uncomfortable, restless, and dissatisfied—I'm going to call that thing purpose.

Have you been feeling like the routine you know isn't good

enough anymore? Maybe you've had a passion buried inside you that's now aching to sprout. That's your purpose calling you, telling you it's time for a shift. Many people die with this purpose unserved, unlived, waiting inside of them in the form of lost dreams, suppressed desires, unnurtured talents, and untapped potential. This usually happens when a person gets caught up in a situation that they don't know how to get out of, or they commit their lives to what seems safe or familiar. In most cases, people spend their lives looking for theirs but never really finding it.

Let me tell you something. Purpose is something we're all born with, and it calls when we're ready to get to that next level in our lives. When you're clear on yours, you can live with confidence in who you are, the role you are meant to play in this world, and the legacy you're destined to leave. For me, I knew mine was more ministry-based. I knew mine was being a real father to my children. I knew it was taking responsibilities of my own, for my own.

Then, there are those who are actively running from and resisting their purpose. Like Jonah, when God told him he was to go to Nineveh or Moses when God told him to speak to Pharaoh, people sometimes think that they can hide from it or that, perhaps, the calling on their life is too big. Some people believe, like Jacob, that they can wrestle it into submission and fit it into their plan for their lives. But the truth is, if you don't honor this calling, the nagging feeling, the emptiness, the pressure—none of it goes away.

The Bible says an unstable man is unstable in all his ways. So, even though you think you're trying to be stable, when you're resistant and out of alignment, you're not stable, and it affects loved ones. You may not realize it, but there are people whose lives depend on you answering your calling, being obedient, and walking in your divine purpose. I don't want to get too deep into it in this chapter, but when you can say yes, God can then work his formula. You see, God has a plan; he doesn't haphazardly put things together. He knew when he created the heavens and Earth. He knew when he created you. Everything under the sun was created with purpose. When you live in yours, you tap into something so much more substantial and fulfilling than you ever imagined.

Over the course of this book, my mission is to help you understand what purpose is and how you can align with yours. When you do, you'll be able to stop waiting, seeking, praying, and wondering. You can have a rich, meaningful life filled with passion and possibility. You will see doors begin to open where you thought there were only walls. You'll be supported in ways you didn't think were probable. And finally, you'll have the stability to walk with confidence, clarity, and a peace that passes beyond all understanding.

In the next chapter, you will get to know a little more about who I am, my journey, and how I came to understand my purpose. As you read my testimony, I hope that you'll be able to reflect on your life and see how purpose has been revealed to you through the people, places, and opportunities that you've found so far.

MY STORY

M y name is Andrae Smith. I've been called by many titles: "Minister," "Prophet," "Bishop." I just like to be called Andrae, sometimes Dre. I am a musician—keyboard player, organist, worship leader, music motivator. And I've worn many hats, being in the church for as long as I have.

For me, this is both a purpose and a calling. (I will explain the difference between these in Chapter 4). I've played music for churches throughout the country, and I've had the honor to share stages with famous artists such as Little Richard and been called to stand in for masters like Billy Preston. You would think that moments like these would be defining points in my career. Although these events were significant and inspiring for me, opportunities for which I will always be grateful, the most fulfilling aspect of my work is not the titles, recognition, or placements, but being a person who can hear and play prophetically for the people who need to receive.

What do I mean when I say, "hear and play prophetically"? The Bible speaks about how there are rivers that flow from heaven. These spiritual rivers are like anointings. God uses several different levels of anointings or dimensions through specific frequencies to connect to people and get his message across. When you go to a church and have a profoundly moving experience from the pastor's message or during the worship session, you have likely experienced one of these rivers from heaven. For these rivers to flow into a service, sometimes someone has to dig a trench.

As a prophetic musician and minister of music, I don't just play songs; I can dig that trench so the pastor can deliver the spiritual waters to the people. Put another way, I can tap into the heart of the ministry, into the essence of the message, and allow my music to paint a picture so that people can have a transcendent experience. This is what I do full-time.

Now, before I go any further into who I am and how I came to be this person, I feel guided to briefly explain the word "anointing" because it will help you understand my journey and the other concepts in this book. Merriam-Webster defines the word anoint as "to smear or rub with oil; however, they also provide a secondary definition, which is "to choose by or as if by divine election." It is this second definition that I want to focus on here.

The Bible references the anointing oil of God, which was used to symbolize and confer God's blessing or divine choice on a person or object. The oil that was used in those days came from an olive. Yes, that shiny, slippery substance people today often cook with was (and still is) used for prayer and religious ceremony. This is so commonplace to us, now, but have you ever stopped to consider how olive oil is actually made?

For the olive to give up its precious oil, in biblical days, it had to be pressed—really pressed. Someone would apply so much pressure to the olive, so intensely, that by the time they finished, what had started as a plump, shiny tasty-looking fruit was crushed beyond recognition. This crushing process would then produce the tiniest drops of oil. Think about that for a moment. To reach its purest form and serve a higher purpose, that olive had to go through a really intense period. If it could think, it probably would have thought it was being killed. But when the process is over, what's left is given power and presence that is used and revered around the world.

Perhaps it is mere circumstance that the chosen anointing oil is produced this way. I like to think that the power of the anointing oil comes from the trial. Likewise, this is how I believe life is. The power of the anointing on someone's life can often be recognized or defined by the intensity of the trial they had to endure to receive it. A similar metaphor is tempered steel. What starts as raw iron goes through a rigorous heating and cooling cycle until it is completely purged of impurity and strengthened to its maximum potential.

I'm explaining this because I am a product of this pressing, tempering process that God sometimes does with us. While I am grateful to be where I am now, my journey today is one that I've had to endure. God had a purpose for me, and more than once, I thought it was too much to handle. More than once, I had to turn back around and ask, "What do I do now?" Someone reading this today may be in such a period, and to you, I say, endure. You will be alright. You are not being destroyed; you are being prepared.

I didn't always understand that anointing, but I was born with it. My mother named me after Andrae Crouch, a legendary gospel writer and singer who's written and published over 1800 gospel songs and hymns that have been played in the church for many years. She was pregnant with me during a time in her life where she was being pressed and pressed to no end. In that pregnancy, the very thing that helped her get through what she was going through was a song that Andrae Crouch wrote called "Take Me Back." The lyrics say, "God, take me back to the place where I first loved you, where it was just me and you. Take me back." What the song was saying was, "God, take away all these other things that are weighing me down. I just want to get back to that personal spot with just me and you."

My mom was so touched that she named me after Andrae Crouch, and she prayed, while I was yet in her womb, that I would touch people's lives like his song had touched hers. To me, this is very deep because the scripture in Jeremiah speaks about how God says he knew us before our parents even got together. He knew us in the womb, and he had a plan for each of us even there, in the womb. And So, as my mom was pregnant with me, she prayed that these things would happen.

I was not born a prodigy. I was born into some dysfunction and things that were pressing me even before I knew what a calling or a gift was. My dad was a pastor, and we lived in the church, literally and figuratively. There was a piano where we lived. With all of the "pressing" happening in my young life, that piano was an outlet for me. After the different services, I found myself in the chapel, and I would gravitate to that piano and start playing some notes. I played what I heard in the services and started playing the notes that I heard in my head.

Throughout the years, my dad's church would host many different events and revival services, which would sometimes draw huge crowds of people and ministers at all levels of the church. I was introduced to many powerful men and women of God, people gifted in the prophetic, people whose prayers and prophecies seemed never to fail. I remember at one of these services, I met a well-known Bishop who prayed for my hands. Not long after that, I can remember being in a revival service, and I could hear the people praising God. Out of nowhere, my ears were opened, and I started to hear the music. It was what we call praise-break or "shout" music, and I could really hear it.

After this service, like many others, I went back to the piano, and I started piecing together what I had heard. Without any lessons, I gained the ability to put the notes together and make chords. I remember the pride I had when. I showed my mom what I had discovered. After that, every time I touched the piano, I was able to play more and more, even things I hadn't heard anywhere. My ears opened to key elements of music and harmony—soprano, alto, and tenor, it all just came.

As an adult, I know that the Holy Spirit was teaching me how to hear these notes, this music from heaven. Before long, my dad started having me play for him, and my gift started to develop. I was started making a difference in the church services. Over the years, I found myself growing and expanding as I gained awareness of my gift. But like I said before, when God has a plan for your life, an anointing for you, it doesn't always come without pressure.

I went through major turmoil at home at a young age, and before I was out of my teenage years, I found myself homeless. I found myself in the streets, in arenas that I wasn't born into, in spaces that I wasn't even allowed to even see on TV (you know, the ones that come on and your parents tell you to close your eyes and turn your head). But there I was in those real-life moments, some of them life-and-death. I began to eat from the forbidden fruit because it was there, and it was what kept me alive, so I thought. I had my gift (that God had given me), but I had a tug to be "in the world" and have my friends "in the world." At the very least, it was safer.

I remember a point where I called myself wanting to join a gang. Being out in the streets, I developed a friendship with a gang set. I loved how they took care of each other, no matter what. For instance, if someone had one dollar, everyone in the group had a piece of it. If that dollar bought a carton of fries, everybody in the house ate, even if it was just one fry. That was the level of love and respect they had for each other. I wanted that. It made more sense than being on my own with no family. So, I told them I wanted to be jumped in. I was ready. I told them I could fight (I couldn't).

Sometimes, as we say in the church, the devil will try to develop some way to get you off of that plan. But we must never forget how God can still take what is meant for evil, as the Bible says, and turn it around for good. When there is a calling on you, it's deeper than just a gift. A calling is like a brand that was placed before you were even born. So, technically, you're branded. No matter what the devil has purposed for you, or whatever you may purpose for yourself, that pressure is only going to come to my good because you're branded.

I asked to join the gang, and they said, "Andrae, we love you. We like you, but we're not going to let you join because you're different. This ain't you." Here's the interesting thing. These men, who outwardly did not know God and didn't go to church, knew that there was a calling on my life. That's the power of the brand. I didn't recognize it. I thought I was abandoned. I was just a kid trying to make it. I was pulled out of school in sixth grade to work in my dad's shop, and I didn't have the know-how to thrive. So, I did what I could and made some mistakes.

I found a girlfriend, got her pregnant, and married her at seventeen years old. I had no idea how to be a father and a husband because my example was not very good. I was also too young to fully understand the depths of the trauma I had lived to that point. I had no business trying to take on anyone else. Although she loved me and would have done anything for me, my young wife already had a purpose and direction for her life. She was already on a path. Because I was out of alignment when I met her, I pulled her out of her purpose, and things didn't go as we had hoped (leading to my opening story).

It wasn't until everything finally came crashing down, and I had nothing—no wife, no kids, no home, no family support—

that I was put on my back and forced to look up. It was in that moment when I was realigned toward my purpose. With nowhere to go but back to the church, I did what I knew how to do, and I played. Sometimes for just ten or fifteen dollars per service or a bundle of food stamps and a place to stay.

It was hard. The struggle was real, as the kids today are saying. But it was during this phase that I started meeting new people who would take me to spaces I never imagined and start to uncover the true depths of my gift. You see, I was uncomfortable, but I was in training. I was being prepared. I didn't have the things I wanted for myself or my kids, but I had what I needed to get by. All the while, my ear was developing. My touch was developing. God was teaching me in every service how spirit flows and making me more comfortable donning the robe he had created for me.

Today, my life is not perfect. I am learning more about my gift and how it manifests in new ways (such as a book). I understand the development of my calling through reflection on the trials I've lived, some of which I am still coming out of. I've come to realize that each trial was a story that God was giving me to make me more humble, compassionate, relatable, and open. He was molding me into a vessel that could contain the anointing that he had placed on my life. My journey isn't over. In fact, the next phase is just beginning. But as I turn the pages on this story, literally and figuratively, I hope that sharing what I've learned so far will help you to get off your back, out of the place of stuckness. I hope to help you endure your pressure so that you, too, can live the purpose that you were created for.

THE JOURNEY

When I was still a child, around fourth or fifth grade, my family and I were living in a church that my father pastored, and I used to have to catch the bus from there to my school on the other side of town. Back then, we didn't have a lot of food at home (the church). We were struggling, and we were no strangers to hunger. So, we only had a certain amount of money available to ensure that I got to school and back.

Next to the bus stop, there was a Taco Bell. Now, one of my favorite foods is a simple bean-and-cheese burrito with "green sauce" and onions. Growing up, it was an inexpensive treat when I had a little extra money. One day after school, I had walked down to the bus stop, and I was hungry. That Taco Bell was right there, and the smell of relief filled my nose. I had just enough change in my pocket (sixty-five cents) to get myself one burrito. But there was a catch. I definitely didn't have any extra money that week, and if I got that burrito, I wasn't going to make it home on the bus. I would have to walk, which would have been devastating for me just from the sheer level of discipline I would receive from my father for missing that bus.

So, my dilemma was, "What do I do?" I decided to get that burrito. The time after I ate that burrito was one of the loneliest and most fearful times of my life to that point. I couldn't get home. I could have stayed in the streets or tried pumping gas for spare change at the new gas station. It didn't matter. Either way, I was in trouble. So, I sat at the bus stop, and I cried. As I sat there wiping tears, trying not to look too defeated, something said, "Just sit here, wait until the bus comes. Maybe somebody's going to let you on." Something else was telling me, "No, that's not gonna happen. You just start walking home now."

In the middle of me sitting there, contemplating and praying, "God, I'm sorry. I knew I shouldn't have done that!" here came this tiny, white pick-up truck with a surfer-looking man driving it. It pulls up to me, and at first, I got scared. What was this guy going to say? Was he going to hurt me?

he rolled down the passenger window and said, "Hey, dude! Hey! God told me to stop here and give you some change."

I went to his window, young and naïve as I was. The man reached down and picked up this big jug full of quarters, nickels, dimes, and half-dollars. He held it up to the window and said, "Take as much as you want here. Take both hands and get as much as you can. The Lord told me to come and give this to you. And to let you know that he loves you."

I stuck my hands in that jar so fast, worried he might change his mind, and grabbed two fistfuls. When I pulled back, the man nodded and pulled away. I never saw him again, but because he showed up, I was standing there with more than enough money to get on the next bus and catch the bus for almost a week. I even had enough to help my parents get a few things from the store like milk and eggs and stuff like that.

As I reflect on this story many years later, I realize that this whole moment had a purpose. My mistake had become a blessing not only to me but to my parents. As I'll explain further in Chapter 4, nothing is without purpose, and God can repurpose anything to serve your highest good. The stranger in the white pick-up truck had a purpose. He was called upon to help me at that moment. He was so confident that God had told him to bless me with that money. What would have happened if he'd chosen to ignore that calling?

You see, sometimes other people depend on you to live your purpose. If that man had not arrived when he did, I could have slept in the streets or walks home. Either way, I was in for a world of discomfort, to say the very least. Because he showed up in a moment of seemingly pure chance, I was spared, and my family was provided for. I don't recall ever saying, "thank you," but I trust that this man has been blessed for his obedience, for answering his call when he heard it. And that is what this book aims to help you to achieve.

No matter your age, race, creed, or experience, you were made with purpose, and throughout life, you will be called to serve in many different ways. I don't intend to tell you what yours is or even the best way to live your life in this book. Instead, my goal is to share my story and what I've learned and hopefully give you one way to start to tap into the still small voice in you so you can understand the nagging and bring an end to the longing and be the person you are destined to be. As such, I just want to provide you with a quick look at the road ahead so you can have an idea of how our journey together looks.

We'll start this journey in Chapter 4, where I dive into the meaning of words like "purpose" and "calling." They are used interchangeably in everyday speech, but for the sake of this book, each one has a specific meaning that will help you to understand what your feeling and what you're meant to do with it. I'll also reveal the first clue to uncovering your purpose.

In Chapter 5, I talk a bit about what it means to have a gift and the power it creates. Sometimes people are gifted but don't understand what that means for them. Know this, your gift gives you presence in spaces where it is most needed; understanding how to use that will help you to find your way.

Similarly, your gift or calling will cause you to have a deep impact on the people you meet and the spaces you enter. In Chapter 6, we will look at how the effect you have on others serves as a clue to what your purpose is.

Once you start to recognize your potential truly, it's time to nurture and cultivate it. In Chapter 7, I share a few insights on connecting with God to sharpen your intuition and expand the depths you can reach when using your gifts. Finally, you'll begin to see how you can interpret for yourself what your calling and purpose are in relation to the tools you've been given.

Chapter 8 talks about how your gift will make room for you and how, once you start to recognize your gift and utilize it, it will position you in places where others cannot go. It will position you in front of great men and give you favor even before your enemies.

After you've come to thoroughly understand your gift, your calling, and how to "tap in," it's time to start moving. In Chapter 9, I go over how to use your gifts and show up with more confidence, intention, and meaning in your life.

Now, we all know the road is not easy. There will be distractions and "shiny object" and traps that the devil will place on your path to try and tempt you away from reaching your fulfillment. This is normal, and sometimes we'll walk right into them. In Chapter 10, I share a little about dealing with distractions so that you don't get too far derailed.

Let's say that you do make a mistake or fall into a trap. What do you do? How do you turn back? Does it mean you have failed?

No! Chapter 11 is dedicated to examining what mistakes are and how to move through them with grace.

Now, sometimes, we don't recognize when we are off the path or headed for destruction. In these times, it's not uncommon for God to put his finger on us and hold us in place. It can feel like we can't move and nothing we try is working, but in reality, something bigger is happening. This is what I talk about in Chapter 12.

In Chapter 13, I talk about forgiveness. In a book about purpose, how can I not? Jesus' whole purpose and message are of forgiveness. He knew we would stumble and backslide, and he forgave us anyway, already. If you are to move past mistakes and into a life of divine purpose, you have to be able to receive and deliver forgiveness.

In Chapter 14, you will learn how to move once you've come to understand your purpose and have fully committed to walking your path (because it is a commitment). Like the man in the truck, you must remain humble enough to hear and be responsible in your duty.

As you walk your path to purpose, you may come across people with similar gifts or callings, and you may be tempted to compare yourself to them. Or you may find that these people become envious of you because of the doors that open to you. In Chapter 15, I talk about how to handle envy and avoid critical comparison.

Finally, in Chapter 16, I just want to remind you of the importance of renewal. You seek a purpose-driven life, one that fulfills you, but remember, that work is not the only thing that will fill your cup. As God rested on the seventh day, so too much you take rests and honor the other facets of your being.

Like I said before, this book is not a manual. I don't expect you to read it and come out knowing exactly how to "do like I do." Actually, I hope that you can avoid some of the things that

I've done after reading this. I am walking more in my purpose every day, but it is a journey. I am not "done." If anything, I'm just a few steps ahead, and that's okay. By the end of this book, you should have a few tools and stories to hold onto that will help you navigate your path. So, I invite you to take this journey with me but encourage you to walk your path according to the guidance you receive in your heart.

4

WHAT IS PURPOSE

What is purpose? What is calling? Like I said in the previous chapter, these two words are often used interchangeably, along with words like meaning and destiny. In this chapter, I hope to illuminate these two words for you because when you look at the definitions, they point to two different aspects of our human experience.

As an elementary illustration, I'd like you to envision a stop sign. It is a red octagon with the word STOP printed in white on the front and screwed to a metal post at the end of a road. Of course, you know exactly what to do when you see one, but I will explain how it works using concepts from this book. The stop sign has the purpose of creating order and saving people from the hazards of a chaotic road. It is uniquely called upon to serve this purpose on roads where it would be impractical to install a stoplight. It accomplishes this purpose by using its gift, which is to immediately grab your attention and deliver the message to "stop."

In this metaphor, the stoplight and the stop sign serve the

same purpose, but the stop sign is called to serve differently based on its unique qualities. That is how purpose and calling work in our lives. In the coming pages, I will dive deeper into what each of these actually means, starting with purpose.

PURPOSE

Merriam-Webster states the definition of the word "purpose" in a few ways:

1. Purpose (*n*) – (**a**) something set up as an object or end to be attained. Intention. (**b**) Resolution. Determination.
Sentence: *Sometimes his life seemed to lack purpose or meaning.*
2. Purpose (*v*) – To purpose as an aim to oneself.
Sentence: *I've been purposing to fix that thing for some time.*

Now, I'd like to share a little scripture with you. While I don't mean for this book to be a dissertation or dissection of the Bible, I think some scripture will help contextualize what I'm going to explain and what all of this together means for us.

In Genesis Chapter 1, God speaks to nothing. Verse 1 says, "In the beginning, God created the heavens and the Earth." God created. He had intention; therefore, this was the first act of purpose. It says the Earth was void, "and darkness was upon the face of the deep." That sounds like most of us. We've all been there, feeling empty, alone, confused, and in a dark place at some point in our lives. In a place where we can't see a future or have hope. At these points, you may ask, "God, do I go left, right, or stay in the middle?" As a person of faith, you may say, "God, I know you have greater for me, but I don't see it." And time is not slowing down. Tick tock. Tick tock.

What's interesting to me is that, while we can sometimes feel like a void and we are running out of time, there is always purpose in what God speaks and does. Looking at the definition of purpose as a verb (which means an action), when God created the heavens and the Earth, he already had a plan. If you read on to verse three of Genesis Chapter 1, the first three words are "And God said." When God spoke his intention, creation happened, and there was light, and there were animals. God purposed for this to happen.

Let's look a little further down to verse 26. "And God said, "Let us make man in our image, after our likeness." Skipping to verse 27, it continues, "So God created man in his own image, in the image of God he created them; male and female." Verse 28 goes on to say, "God blessed them. And God said to them, 'Be fruitful and multiply.'"

Let's pause and review real quick. In the first lines, God "purposed" (the verb) the heavens, Earth, and all creation. He had his intention, and the last lines give us a clue into what that was. Remember, purpose as a noun means something set up as an object or end to be attained. Genesis Chapter 2 says God formed man of the dust of the ground. He used the initial creation to produce the final one, humanity. So, in other words, God's purpose in this was to create humanity—us! We are God's plan. You are walking and talking purpose. How cool is that? What's more, not only is our purpose (the noun) to exist, but he gave us specific intention, a precise aim for why we exist.

As one more piece of scriptural evidence, let's look at Isaiah 14:24. "The Lord of hosts has sworn (made an oath) 'As I have planned, so shall it be; and as I have purposed, so shall it stand." For the believer, this is proof that God created it all with purpose and has assigned purpose to us. If you are not a person of faith or are on the fence about religion right now, that is okay. What I hope you can take away from this is that you are not here without intention. You are a product of what God is doing. You are purpose.

I know it may sound a little self-centered, but it is not. I'm reminded of something my nine-year-old daughter, Laila, said while with her mother not that long ago. My daughter's last name is Smith. Her mother's last name is Frasier. Her sister's last name is Frasier. Somehow, a conversation came about wherein she was named or responded to as a Frasier. Laila had to correct them by reminding them she is not a Frasier but a Smith. ("Get it right.") Saying this was not to take away from the name or heritage of Frasier, but she had to establish her identity. You are God's purpose. You are God's identity. ("Let us make man in our image.")

Have you ever noticed that the Bible frequently uses a person's lineage as are introduced? This established purpose, authority, power, or rite (and right) of passage. What you are called, and even more so what answer to, is a sign of the power, potential, and position you can claim. Many people and entities will try to name you something other than who you are to limit your potential.

Here's a modern example that might bring a little clarity to this "names" and "rights" concept. If you were to go to the White House right now and try to walk in, uninvited, you would get turned away, possibly even arrested. But if you were to go to the White House with an invitation or badge declaring your name, purpose, and right to be there, you would be granted access. Claiming your identity as the purpose of God gives you the right to exist in your purpose, to prosper as he has intended, and to fulfill any specific role he has assigned to you. You're not a visitor here on Earth; you were assigned here.

So, have you been trying to figure out what your purpose is? Why are you here? What should you be doing? What is purpose? The answer is simple; you are purpose, God's word living and breathing. Perhaps you are struggling because you are looking in all of the wrong places.

I was reading a blog the other day, and the writer was recollecting a story in a book he had read. In the book he read, a man was sent to a gulag in the old Soviet Union, where he struck up a friendship with another prisoner. He told his friend about the family and career he left at home and his plans to return to them after his twenty-five-year sentence was up.

The other prisoner stopped him and said, "Look, this is Gulag, not many leave here alive. You do not know if you will be alive tomorrow. If you are to survive, you must think about what is important."

The man asked his friend what was more important than his family and career, and the older prisoner said, "The present—the here and now. You and me talking, forming a friendship, a bond. That is what is most important."

The moral of that story is perhaps people do not find their purpose because they are too focused on the future even though God says he has our futures set up already. When you realize that in reality, we are the purpose and that it's just the blueprint that we cannot see, we can pray, "God, show me your plans for my life," knowing that God has a daily plan that leads to an expected end. That expected end is fulfillment, rest, peace, love, joy, abundance, overflow, more than enough, and divine favor. Jeremiah 29:11 says, "'For I know the plans I have for you,' declares the Lord, 'plans of good and not evil, to give your future and a hope.'" This, my friend, is purpose.

CALLING

You may have heard this word and thought you knew what it meant. But as I explained with my stop sign analogy, it is different from purpose, meaning, or destiny. To me, calling is more spiritual. While many people, beings, or systems may share a similar or related purpose, a calling is personal. It calls you out, defines you, and separates you from others. When you're called to something, you have been chosen and branded with divine approval and a mission only you can fulfill.)

Sometimes I picture it as a mother who is looking for her child and doesn't know that the child is playing hide and seek. She's calling and calling, thinking that this child is lost. Then when she finally finds the child, a connection is sparked, and the mother just loves on them and says, "Oh, I thought you were lost. I thought I could never get to you." For the Christian, this is how it is when we answer the calling that's been placed on us.

Sometimes, there's a calling that takes a person to a higher level. This higher calling may even set you apart and above others who are talented, qualified, and gifted because you were called, not them. (I'll talk more about this in Chapter 15.) The reason is that he planted a seed in you that he wants to bear fruit. (To whom much is given, much is required). So, that calling is God yearning for you, as the mother for her child. And just as he wants more for you, he wants something more from you that he may not want from your neighbor.

For instance, for me, there's a calling of ministry through music. Some people may have that calling from ministry, and some people may have a gift of music. I'm one of the people who have both. I love to play music, all kinds of music, in different arenas. Gospel. Jazz. R&B. Classical. Neosoul. I love to see the people respond to how the energy of the music. I also love to see how people react to the ways God uses me in the church. To a certain level, there is a calling of ministry because I'm only able to play music. After all, God is speaking to me and telling me the types of notes to play for that service.

You may have heard people say there's a calling on your life. You may be a musician like me, or you may be an usher. You may think you're working your calling when, in fact, you are working your gift. One of your giftings may be to be an usher. One of your giftings may be to be a musician. A gift is a divine seed planted in you, such as playing music, speaking in public, writing books, or even having a dazzling smile. Your gift is the quality that you bring to the work you do because you are uniquely talented in that arena.

Your calling is different. If God is calling you to something, it goes deeper than how you express your gift. If you want to know what your calling is, you can be sure it will most likely have something to do with ministry. It would be something that brings people to him, spiritually speaking. You may be called to heal, save lives, or inspire transformation, but it will always bring people in one way or another to a state that is closer to God. This doesn't have to be in the church directly, either. Sometimes it means being in spaces that don't seem to know God at all. This is where your unique testimony, your trial, becomes your treasure and your pain becomes your purpose. You may have a story that grants you access to people that even the most renowned men and women of God cannot reach.

For instance, I can play at a service on Sunday morning and then do a gig at a bar in the evening. Some people would think, "Wow, Andrae. How can you go here and play this worldly music?" What they don't realize is that by having me in these spaces, God has an inside man with the people who may not be going to church. I can have a heart-to-heart conversation with someone who needed healing that hasn't seen a church in years. I can play the right note or say the right word or give the right smile for them to release something they'd been holding. I may never know how my gift will be used, but if I show up and ask God to use me for his purpose, I can trust that he will use me. The music is the gift, the conduit for answering my calling or assignment and serving my purpose.

I want to close this chapter with a dream I had years ago when God called me for more ministry. My father, being a minister, was known as a deliverance pastor at the time, and I had joined up under his ministry. One night, I had a dream that I was playing on the organ. The saints of God were rejoicing in my father's preaching, and he was laying hands on people and deliverance was going forth. And there I was playing. As I played, the organ seemed to be rising up above the church. The more I played, the higher that organ and I rose. Before I know it, I was looking down on the congregation because I'd been lifted so high on my instrument.

Eventually, as the organ rose higher still, it started tilting to the left, and it reached the point where I could not keep playing because I was trying to hold on to the organ. It wasn't long before I couldn't hold on, and I fell off the organ and onto the altar. When I got to the altar, right where my father was preaching, he handed me the mic, and I began to preach and lay hands on people. To me, it doesn't get any clearer than that.

To me, this dream is significant for a couple of reasons. First, it's an example of how God tries to show us our callings. God had shown me the sign in a dream. How has he offered you a sign? In what ways could he be speaking to you right now? Are you listening? (I'll talk more about this in Chapter 7.)

Sometimes we pretend to have missed the sign. Why? Sometimes the calling just seems too unpleasant, like Jonah being sent to Nineveh or too big, like Moses being told to go to Pharaoh. Sometimes it doesn't line up with our own plans. We like to create our own destinies even though sometimes the destinies we envision don't have our best interests in mind. I was like this. I was afraid, like Moses. I was comfortable on the organ and the piano. God was asking me to use my voice, and eventually, I did, but I resisted for a long time. This book is just another instance of this calling coming back to me, urging me to reach deeper.

If you are looking for a more fulfilled and meaningful life, my message to you now is to reach deeper and explore the depths of your calling. Think about the gifts you have and how you have been using them? How had you served others? How can you serve more? People are the purpose, and if you're to answer your calling, you may have to find out how you are going to impact people. This is what I cover in the following chapters.

5

GIFTS, POWER, & PRESENCE

The last chapter explained the first two major concepts to understanding your God-given purpose: purpose and calling. As I said before, you are the purpose. People are the purpose. And the calling is an assignment to be of service to people and bring them closer to God. In this chapter, I want to look at three more concepts through which you will actually begin to accomplish what you are called to do: gifts, power, and presence.

I'll explain each of them in-depth, but to help you make sense of this, I want to give you the "CliffsNotes." Like I said before, your gift is like a seed meant to bear fruit at the right time. It is divinely purposed as a conduit through which you can answer your calling. The power of this gift comes through God's anointing, and it's up to each of us to use it responsibly. Using your gift in its highest purpose will give you a presence that draws the people who need you. Let's go deeper.

GIFTS

When I was a child, Christmas was one of my favorite holidays. It was a festive time, and I remember being filled with wonder and hope seeing houses dressed up in colorful Christmas lights, with their bright, ornamented trees glowing in the windows. The image of the fireplace burning and the family gathered around listening to Nat King Cole and singing songs is still planted in my mind. At this time of year, it got just cold enough in Southern California for this to be a pleasant thought (as opposed to summertime when there was no escape from the heat). Christmas time just had that special thing for me.

One of the most exciting and memorable things about Christmas, for me, was knowing that my mom was going to "throw down" in the kitchen. For anyone who doesn't know what throw down means, it means mom was going to cook really, really good for Christmas. I knew that we would have all kinds of homemade desserts—sweet potato pies, pecan pies, cookies, German chocolate cake, coconut cake, banana cakes—all of these different sweets. We would have the dressing and the baked chicken and the black-eyed peas and all of that stuff. My mom was good.

Me being an eater, a person who loves food, I wanted to stay around that kitchen. I knew when mom got done with those pies, that chocolate cake, or whatever it was, I was going to have first dibs at licking the spoon and bowl. It was going to be "on and cracking!" For me, food was everything. So, Christmas was an extra special time.

The second thing that was exciting to me was knowing that there would be a gift under the tree for me. I would always feel like it was going to be something that I wanted. Even though, as I found out when I got older, we were going through tough times, my mom and dad would try to make it feel special, and they always stressed gratitude. I probably wouldn't get everything on my wish list, but the fact that I could make that list, and maybe— if I hoped and prayed—they would have the money to at least get me one of those things, kept the excitement alive. They would say, "Well, we can't get everything on your list. You know, but just be grateful for whatever you get." To me, that was preparation. They were letting me know I might not get anything, but I still had that anticipation because there would still be a gift under that tree with my name on it, wrapped in colorful paper and topped with a bow. And I knew that it meant something for them, especially for my mother, to get it for me. And so that anticipation for that gift is everything.

I remember, one Christmas, I was excited to open a big box that was waiting for me. I had put all the things I wanted on the list—the GI Joe, the Andre the Giant wrestling figure, the Voltron from the TV series. Most of the younger readers won't recognize Voltron, but anyone in my generation will. Voltron was the coolest toy on the market. He had this sword, and all of the pieces had to come together to form this big robot figure. I wanted Voltron. So, I was eyeing this box and thinking, "This might be the Voltron in there."

On Christmas day, I ripped the paper off and opened the box. What I lifted it up was not Voltron, but a ski jacket, a winter coat. I remember thinking, "Okay, all right. I see the winter coat. That's nice, but where's the Voltron? Let me keep digging." The next item was a sweater, and all I could do was hear my mom saying, "Oh, isn't that nice? I hope you can fit it."

I kept digging and... shoes. I tried to keep a smile on my face because I knew it meant a lot to her just to be able to get us some clothes. When Christmas came, we got clothes to set us up for when school started back our next school year. That was everything for her, being able to take care of us. Inside, I was disappointed, but I did not want to show it.

I feel like God is similar to my parent when he gives us gifts. See, my mom would give us (my brothers and sisters and me) something that we may not want at the time, but it would be something that would cover us at just the right time. As a little boy at Christmas time, I wasn't thinking about that ski jacket, the sweater, or any of that stuff. But the morning I had to go to school, it was raining (and back then we had to walk to school most often), I was grateful to be prepared. And when I went to school in my new shoes, and people would notice, I liked the clout from that. It made me feel good. Mom made sure that I had the things that would take care of me.

God is the same way. He gives gifts, and in these gifts, there's purpose. You may not see it right away because you want something else that seems cooler or more exciting, but in reality, that gift will have everything that you wanted, and you'll appreciate it when the true purpose becomes clear. His gifts are set up to equip you for what your future holds. For example, you may have the gift of words. You're a master of words. When you're young, the other kids with talents like singing and music and sports may all seem cooler. But God wasn't preparing you to be cool on the fourth-grade playground. He was preparing you for the college entry exams and the books you may write and speeches you may give that inspire a generation.

Here's another example. I don't read music. I was never classically trained, so I never became fluent in that style of playing. I could look at this and think that others got a better gift than me. I could covet the ability to read and write. But I don't have to. The gift that I have wasn't for me to flex my knowledge of music theory; it was to make an immediate impact. When pastors need a musician who can flow and understand music ministry, they know that I am gifted in that arena, and they call me.

POWER

"To whom much is given much is required." (Luke 12:48)

I love superhero movies. It's always been interesting to me how the superhero becomes the superhero. One of my favorites heroes was always Incredible Hulk. I loved his character because he was so strong, and if anybody were to attack him or get them angry enough, he knew how to deal with them. If he was being bullied or treated wrong, he had the power to stop it, which was something I connected with growing up. I wanted to be able to do that, to feel powerful like Hulk was.

Before he became the powerhouse superhero, the Hulk's real name was Dr. Bruce Banner, and he was a scientist who worked with radiation. He got trapped in an accident in his work which exposed him to extreme amounts of radiation—lethal levels that should have taken him out. I want to pause here because there's somebody reading this now who, like Dr. Banner or myself even, may have been in a situation that was so toxic that you've got this radiation of issues around you that should have taken you out spiritually or physically or mentally. You should have walked away from the situation handicapped. What I want you to know is that even in the midst of that, God had a plan. What was meant to destroy you has been repurposed for your good.

Dr. Banner went through that traumatic event—in his case, a literal explosion—but miraculously, he came out unharmed. And the next time he was attacked or felt misused, he trans-formed into the Incredible Hulk. Then, when he changed back into himself, the person he recognized, he was confused because everything had changed and been rearranged.

God's power is like that. Just like the radiation came over Dr. Banner suddenly and filled him with the power to change things, so it is with God's anointing. It sweeps over us, protecting us from things that would destroy others and imbuing us with the power of God. Power to create. Power to transform.

Now here, with the realization of this power, Dr. Banner had to make a choice. He had all of this incredible strength and no one to stop him, and he could have chosen to become a villain. Fortunately, he did not. He chose to do the right thing and protect people (answering his calling).

I'm reminded of a Biblical hero who, after receiving his power made the wrong choice. Do you remember David, the ruddy shepherd boy who slew the Giant, Goliath, with a sling? Before he was a hero, David was no one special in the world's eyes. He was small in stature and tended to sheep. He was the boy who would have had to make the sandwiches for his brothers. His only notable qualities at the time were that he could play music—beautiful music—but he was not famous or celebrated. Still, this was who God anointed to be the next king.

That anointing covered him and helped him to slay Goliath. It gave him recognition among the people to where they went around saying Saul (the present king) slew his thousands and David slew his ten-thousands. This anointing caused an issue of jealousy, which I'll talk about in a later chapter. For now, it's just important to recognize that sometimes even as your anointing lifts you, there will be those who plot against you. Despite this, David still became one of the greatest kings.

But David was still a man, and he made mistakes, using his power selfishly sometimes. He saw the woman Bathsheba in the bath and decided he wanted to be with her. He slept with her, and she became pregnant. The problem was, Bathsheba was a married woman, and David should not have been with her. Instead of being honest with God, David misused his power again and decided to have her husband killed to cover up his transgression.

When you are anointed with the power of God, you have a responsibility to use that in service. You are expected to benefit others. God's anointing doesn't just have the potential to change your life but the lives of all the people who may depend upon you living your purpose!

The Bible says that it's the anointing that breaks the yoke. For those who don't know, a yoke a wooden crosspiece fixed around the necks of two animals and attached to the plow or cart that they are to pull. It is a tool of bondage. To have that anointing on your life is to have the power to break chains and bring people out of bondage. That is what it is for. As you seek to answer your calling and live in alignment with your purpose, think about ways you have exhibited power to create this kind of change in your life and the lives of others. Maybe you're the type of person that speaks, and everyone listens. Maybe, if you're a musician like me, people come to you after you play and tell you how you've touched them. That is your clue!

I realized the power of my anointing while playing for a funeral when I was younger. It was one of the first funerals I had the opportunity to play for by myself, and I had been asked to play a song on the organ, just one organ solo. Being young and untrained, I thought, "What's the most popular funeral song?" At the time, it was "Precious Lord." It was a song filled with sorrow just for funerals, so I played that song. That was when I had my superhero moment.

I played the organ so hard and really drove it in. I drove and drove and drove because my mentality was not about helping this family through bereavement. I didn't realize the song, itself, was so loaded with intensely emotional elements in the lyrics and the tones, so I kept playing, driving in the power of the music. Performing. I was thinking about how good I must look and how these people would remember me playing.

Before had finished the song, the mother of the child that

had passed away stood up and began screaming and hollering and hyperventilating, and it disrupted the whole service. They had to call an ambulance because she was having an asthma attack. And my initial thing was, "Wow... Look at how much power I got.... The power is in my hand!" I didn't realize that in that instance, I was the villain. I was supposed to help these people, but my heart was not focused on that.

It wasn't until the funeral directors came and said, "Andrae, we will never hire you to do a funeral again. You messed up this funeral!" that I realized I had done something wrong. After that, I had to shift my focus and use the power in my hands for its anointed purpose: to help people.

PRESENCE

Once you realize that you're gifted and you recognize your anointing, presence is very simple. You know God is everywhere, and if God is in this anointing that he bestowed on you, then that means he's in you. This means that you now have to have a level of confidence within yourself. You have to have the awareness, "I am who God made me." You are a help and not a hindrance. As the Bible says, you are the head and not the tail, the lender and not the borrower. Once you know these things—your gift, your power, and where your anointing comes from, and where that power comes from—they will automatically cause a presence or aura to come over you that allows you to walk in confidence and authority.

I know that as Andrae Smith, and knowing who God is in my life, when I walk into a room as a minister of music, the atmosphere already starts changing. Even if people don't recognize it yet, I know it's changing. If I know if I'm about to do with anything that has to do with my gift, I can be confident that when I enter the room, then something has to shift. You may feel that when you go to certain places or when a certain minister or teacher walks in the space, and something about them makes you want to really listen to what they say. You have to know where the gift and power come from, and then the presence will follow.

6

THE IMPACT YOU LEAVE

There is a scripture that talks about being living epistle. It actually says, in 2 Corinthians 3:

> "Ye are our epistle written in our hearts, known and read of all men: Forasmuch as ye are manifestly declared to be the epistle of Christ ministered by us, written not with ink, but with the Spirit of the living God; not in tables of stone, but in fleshy tables of the heart."

I had to look up the word "epistle" when I first heard it as a young teenager to understand this. An epistle is a letter or a book written in letters. In this chapter, Paul the Apostle writes to the church in Corinth, and he starts by asking if he and his followers (early Christians) needed to establish their credentials through new letters of recommendation. While this was common practice for traveling teachers and ministers in new cities, Paul points out that papers and letters are not what is needed to prove the power or presence of God in their ministry. Rather, it was their lives and their impact.

While there are a few ways to interpret these verses, the one that sticks with me now is that our lives are open books to people. This is important because what is in that book is how you impact people. People will read your book (your life) and see who you are and the nature of your heart. They will see your anointing by how you carry yourself and know you (the God in you) by the way your story—your epistle—changes them. And they will remember,

As I'm writing a part of my journey in this literal book, I want to remind you that your book doesn't always have to have good stories. Everything doesn't have to out like peaches and cream in your book (life) to mean something to someone else. Just the opposite can be true. You may have many chapters of stress, of making mistakes, and of enduring problems. But for the believer, there is also evidence of how God comes into your life gets you through those problems when you let him be the forefront. He says, "Come unto me all that are heavy-laden, and I will give you rest," which is vital because strength and a sound mind are important to working in your gift.

My life is a living epistle read of by men. What is in your book? Whatever people "read" and receive in your book is your legacy. For instance, when people encounter me, I've noticed that they seem to light up. They see my smile and feel my love for God and for what I do. Even without hearing anything in my story, they can feel its weight and know that I'm genuine. Sometimes we talk, and I tell people pieces of my journey, and they come away maybe a little inspired because my smile is proof that, even after trials, you can survive. This is my legacy. But that is only a taste of my impact.

Being a musician and never having any lessons, playing strictly through the anointing of God, my life is my legacy. This life of music has been my legacy. As I live it, people are able to see that and connect spiritually. They can connect and know there's something deeper than just what's on the outside. There's something more profound than just being a musician.

To me, this is deep because God doesn't make anything ordinary. You see, many great musicians have dedicated many hours of practice to their craft, improving gradually as they put in the hours. This is called discipline and it can take you far in life, especially as a musician or an artist. It takes major discipline to sit down and learn how to play the piano or the organ—any instrument for that matter. But for me, learning to play was not a result of hours of labor but an anointing. I was blessed to operate in this gift extraordinarily, without any training. That's what makes it different from a skill.

Of course, later on in life, I had to learn if I wanted to get better. To go further, I had to take the talent that God gave me and not bury it but try to reproduce it and learn how to make it work for me. Still, the gift is in his anointing, and when he does something, he doesn't make ordinary. He makes extraordinary, which causes people to look and be amazed. It reminds me of the peacock.

If you look at the peacock without it flexing his feathers, it's just a large bird. But when he shows its colors, you can't help but notice and say, "Whoa! Look at all the beautiful colors." That's how God's anointing shows up in our lives. We operate extraordinarily. But it's not simply to make us look good. Remember, the gift and anointing have a higher purpose, and so people who see it are moved. Your gift is extraordinary—it needs to be—because it must be able to touch people deeply and strike a chord that others with a similar talent can't. So, you must know that the colors that God gave you are so unique, so spiritually dialed in that they are going to affect people in the places where they sometimes can't see color, where the people may be spiritually colorblind. And all of it with the purpose of touching their hearts.

This is what God wants to do. The gift he placed in you is the ability to reach out and touch the hearts of people. Everything with spirituality is really about the heart. What's in your heart? It's about changing your heart to reflect the God in you and changing others' hearts to become temples for God to live in them. What is in your heart will always come out, and if it's not in the right place, you won't be able to make the impact you need to make on others for them to align with their purpose. You know, when you walk in your purpose, you will often be the exact answer to someone else's prayer—and you may never know it! That is the power of alignment.

God blessed me to play extraordinarily and supernaturally in funerals, which are very touchy services. They have a sensitive atmosphere, different from weddings and gatherings on Sunday mornings because you're dealing with people whose hearts have already broken. The attendees may be dealing with depression, hurting from guilt over a poor relationship with the deceased, facing anger toward other relatives as old emotions are stirred up. But God allows me in my music to come and impact these people if I let him. I can go in and be an ordinary musician and just play the songs on the list as they are, with no emotion or heart, because I don't know these people. But when God gives you a gift, you're the conduit. The blessing is for the people. I can do more for them than playing the song.

I think about it like electricity. When they build a house, there are all these wires (that most people never see) called conduits. These wires have to carry the electrical power. The power has to flow through them to become accessible at the power outlets. But the cables and outlets are not the power sources; it's coming from somewhere else. You can think of the funeral service as an outlet, where people plug in to receive healing grace. As the anointed conduit, I carry that charge (I've also been charged with that responsibility), but I'm connected to a source that doesn't come from me.

If I remember to use this connection, I can bring light to this family's dark situation. The people who are despondent and walking in darkness, in a place of spiritual colorblindness, will hear, receive, and remember how the music lifted them up. For someone reading this book now, your gift may just be a beautiful, sincere, warm smile. People don't understand why or how you smile the way you do, but it makes them want to smile too. Or maybe you have an infectious laugh. Perhaps you have the gift of compassion. That is a gift because not everyone can reach deep into their heart and share sincere kindness with people in a time of need.

I'm reminded of a time where I played for a funeral for an older gentleman. His wife, to whom he'd been married for almost 65 years, had just passed, and it really hurt him to his heart that she died before him. I had to make sure that I was able to tap into the type of music he needed to hear that would touch him in his time frame. I couldn't go in there and play anything, like the new age Kirk Franklin. He wouldn't relate to Kirk. But he related to Amazing Grace. I didn't know the family to know that song meant something to him and to his wife. But I played it.

About a year or so later, I played at a regular service for the same church. On my way out to my car after service, a car pulled up on the side of me. A younger gentleman was driving. In the passenger's seat, lo and behold, there was the husband who lost his wife. He said, "Hey brother, Andre. Man, I was just so happy to see you. You remember you played for my wife's funeral."

Now, I play for so many funerals, so it took me a minute to just remember. But as he began to talk, it started coming back. "Yes. Yes, I do, brother. It's good to see you."

And he said, "You sang that song. Me and my wife, we loved that song, and it really touched me."

Wow. I don't consider myself a singer, but God told me to open my mouth and sing that day. And with God's anointing, he makes things so big and so beautiful. When he touches you to do one thing, it illuminates. So, this family may not have heard cracked notes or any special runs on the keys. What they heard was, "I've had some good days, I've had some bad days, but I won't complain." Like the song says. And that is what the man needed at the time.

I could see his eyes starting to tear up as he was talking. He also had this brown paper bag in his hand, like a lunch sack. He said to me, "Me and my grandson saw you, and I was hoping I got a chance to get to you. I think it was meant for you to be in this parking lot right now." They had apparently been stalling, hoping that they could catch me. He gave me the paper bag and told me not to open it until I got in the car and drove off because that was for me. Then they left.

I did as he said and waited until I was in my car and had driven a little way down the road. Just like I did at Christmas, I felt all this anticipation and excitement. What could he have put in that bag for me? Was it going to make me smile? When I got a little distance between the church and me, I opened the bag and see that it's just full of money: twenties, fifties, fives, and tens— over $400. I didn't expect that at all, but I couldn't be more grateful because I needed it at the time.

Think about this with me for just a moment. This man was so moved by the way my music, my gift, touched him that a whole year later, he found me and wanted to bless me. That is the power of walking in your purpose. This story highlights two major points about purpose. First, the people who need you receive something special, and they will remember. This goes beyond meeting a star or celebrity or someone they admire. When you show up and meet their needs, they are profoundly changed and, like the Samaritan woman who met Jesus at

Jacob's well, will be compelled to talk about the blessing they just received. As living epistles, we show God's spirit through our lives, and people respond to that. Second, though you may not recognize it all the time, when you're in alignment, doing what you're called to do obediently, sincerely, you will be taken care of. Your needs will be met, and the blessings you give come back around.

Before I close this chapter, I want to invite you to think about when, where, and how you have been the most impactful to the people you meet. What have people received from you that they can't stop talking about? If you listen closely, people will tell you what your gift is. If you have a spirit of teaching, people may tell you that when you speak, everything becomes more apparent. If you have a gift of healing, people may open up to you in ways that they don't with others without even knowing why. If you're an artist, people may tell you that the way you use colors or capture features just inspires them and makes them feel.

Where people are profoundly moved, where they feel deeply impacted, that is where your gifting lies. And where you find your gift, there to will you find clues to your calling. In the next chapter, I will share with you how to start tapping into the divine nature of your gift.

7

LEARNING TO HEAR GOD

I love documentaries. I especially love documentaries about musicians and music icons. As a musician myself, I always feel a connection to their stories because sometimes I can relate. Sometimes I learn something about artists I looked up to and realize that we share a particular gift or quality. Sometimes it's just really inspiring to see how someone becomes who we know them to be. I'm not one of those nosey folks who just want to know all the scandals. While it can be exciting and even moving to learn about the person's trials, it means more to me to hear about how they triumphed. What did they go through, and how did they come out of it?

During the time that I was writing this book, I watched a documentary on Mahalia Jackson. For those who don't know her by name, Mahalia Jackson is an outright legendary gospel singer, one of the most famous and influential gospel singers of the 20th century. She was also very active in the Civil Rights movement and sang "Precious Lord" at Dr. Martin Luther King's funeral. As I watched her journey to becoming this person, I could not help but see parallels between her story and the topics I was writing about.

You see, Mahalia had this voice that made her perfect for jazz. It was big. It was powerful. It had range. When she sang, you could feel the emotion of what she was singing. Many musicians wanted her, pushed her to sing jazz music, but that was not what inspired her. She had no passion for just jazz or, especially, the blues. She felt a tug toward happier things, towards life and ultimately gospel music.

Mahalia Jackson started out singing in the church, and the spirit that she had grew. Her passion for that kind of music was nurtured until she didn't want to do anything else. She had found a purpose there in that style, in the messages, in the frequencies, and in the energy. She knew that she had a calling there. Her talent, her gift, was so passionate in gospel that she would not change even though she was coveted and chased after by other big names. Even though she could have been a mega-star just from singing just alone, she knew what she was supposed to be doing. Because she listened to that and used her gift confidently, which we'll talk about in Chapter 9, she was able to become legendary in gospel and *still* earn incredible respect in jazz.

Even for her, the road wasn't easy. She had to miss some deals in the beginning. She had to say no to things that didn't affirm her spirit. She had to have clarity and trust even though the people around her were trying to tell her her purpose and what she could be if she listened to them. She needed to tune in to what she knew inside constantly, and because she could do that, she became one of the first gospel artists to go double-platinum. Way back in the 40s and 50s, this was unheard of. Most gospel artists, to this day, haven't even been able to achieve this or anything close.

The question that I'm sure many people were asking was, "Mahalia, how do you know?" How did she know she would be great in gospel? How did she know jazz was not for her? How did she know she would make it in her way versus listening to the promoters and the agents? To me, it is clear. Ms. Jackson was in *alignment*.

Merriam-Webster defines the word align as "to bring into a line or agreement" and "to be in or come into precise adjustment or correct relative position." To be in alignment means to agree, to have the correct positioning and orientation. What Mahalia Jackson had was the proper orientation so to be able to hear and agree with the spirit of God in her and tune out everything that did not agree with that.

This is a powerful lesson for us as we seek to answer our callings and live our purpose. I read a post on social media the other day that said, "Don't tell everyone your calling. It was not a group call." I laughed, but it is true. God won't plant the seed of your purpose in anyone else but you. So, you must be the one to tend that seed until it can bear fruit. I'm not saying that people cannot serve as confirmation and that people won't tell you what your true purpose is. In fact, they often will. But you must learn to hear with your spiritual ears to have the discernment to know who or what is and is not for you. To do this, you must learn to build a connection with God.

Being a musician in the church, it was very vital for me to learn how "flow" and play the right kinds of music, the right styles of music that would be effective for the service. The first time that I homed in on that was as a young boy. Because my father was a pastor, I attended a Christian school, and there was this book that we had from the curriculum, which was called ACE. I remember the book talking about the types of careers we wanted to go into, and one of the careers was a musician. I thought this was so cool because most of the books in school don't have that as an option. They talk about doctors and engineers, but the full-time musician—I had never heard that I could take that path, especially in the form of a church musician. I remember that sticking to me right off the bat.

Later, we had to do a lesson on the importance and role of the church musician or the organist, which I was learning to be at my dad's church. What ministered to me and stuck with me from that lesson was that the musician prepares and softens people's hearts before ministry comes forth. This is the *purpose* of the church musician, and it set the tone for me and how I would come to play.

Sometimes I would drift from this, like at the funeral home, and I would focus on myself instead of people's hearts. Sometimes, I needed a sign or nudge in my heart to remind me of this. Sometimes, I've been so into what I was doing that an in-tune pastor has looked back at me and told me to change the music because he needed something that flowed with him. That's how important being in the right spirit is. Imagine my feeling, being called out in front of the entire congregation—not in a disrespectful way, of course, but recognizing that for that moment, the service had to stop. The attention was on me to get back into alignment instead of on bringing people to God.

The other thing the book mentioned that I eventually learned from experience was to prepare myself. A musician should always pray before they play. What this does is calms your spirit and tunes you into the atmosphere of the crowd. It attunes you the frequency that God needs you to be on. For me, this allows me to get out of the way and let the power flow through me as the conduit. I can be the one to dig the trench and touch people's hearts, but I have to listen to be able to hear God speaking to me.

That is the point of this chapter. You know that that people are the purpose. You know that if you are called, you have an assignment, mission, or calling to be of service in some way. You know that the gifts you have will give you the power to touch people's hearts and lives, and with that, the responsibility to take care of them and point them back to the source. This is the path of purpose, in a sense. You cannot effectively walk this path if you first don't attune your eyes, ears, and spirit to hear God directing you. There are a few things that you need to know to help you strengthen your connection with God.

CLEAR THE CHANNEL

Have you ever listened to the radio, and there was a ton of static? Or have you tried to have a conversation, but there's too much background noise in the room? Sometimes the conversation with God is like that because there is too much "stuff" in the background. This stuff can be people in your life who constantly need attention, to the point that they become distractions. It can be your own thoughts. Our minds are always so busy, and that is truer now with so much technology. TVs, smartphones, internet radio, work, errands—we have all these things that can take our attention at any moment, and before we know what happened, we have lost hours.

To strengthen the connection and hear what's coming through, you have to cut out some of the chatter. Take time for yourself to be in prayer and meditation. I'm not saying you have to go out into the wilderness and fast for forty days as Jesus did. But think about your daily life. Do you have a moment of peace and silence in the morning before starting your day, or do you roll out of bed and get right to work or start taking care of the kids? When you get home, do you take a moment to turn off the phone or put it away, or do you get home and still take work calls? When you have your days off, do you ever just sit with yourself in silence for a few minutes, or do you spend all your time catching up on things you couldn't do before?

If you are always doing something, you never have room to listen. Thoughts, especially anxious ones, are noisy things. Too many of them get in the way. Just like I have to take a moment to pray before playing, I have to take time out of my day to pray and be still. The conscious act of clearing clutter from the channel, little bits at a time, will help you get more in tune.

KEEP IT 100

Some of the clutter I mentioned isn't stray thoughts and outside obligations but internal hurdles. These hurdles often take the form of secrets and things done in the dark that we are ashamed of, habits that we have not yet let go of. To have a clear channel, you have to have transparency. You must be honest with yourself. This is the number one thing you will need to line up straight with God.

I remember as a kid, my brothers and I used to share a room. Imagine three or four boys in one room—it was a mess! Mom would tell us to clean our room, and, being young boys, we took the obvious shortcuts. Kick things under the bed. Stuff what you can in the closet. The room would look real nice the next time mom came around... until she opened the closet, and all of our junk came falling out.

What you throw in the closet piles up, and it keeps piling up until you deal with it. If you try to hide your dirty laundry, it doesn't go away. God already knows you put it in the closet. The thing is, he needs you to have a clean room and a clean closet. He's going to give you things to save in for later, and you'll need to pull them from the closet. It would help if you cleared the old stuff out. You must clean your inner space up. This means getting real with yourself.

As a young man, do you have a problem with chasing women? Do you have trouble keeping your word? Do you have a problem showing up on time when you're called upon? As a young lady, have you been addicted to the attention of different men? Have you been deceitful with friends? As a parent, have you been overly harsh with your children, even after you've promised yourself to ease up?

When you start trying to line up with God, he's going to open that closet and tell you to deal with these things. You'll need the courage to face yourself. What you face, you can own. What you own, you can defeat. You don't have to get it all done at once. God knows each of us is a work in progress. But pay attention to yourself and how you're living. Confess with your mouth the error of your ways and ask for forgiveness when you mess up. Make a conscious effort to be better each day. Know that you have someone who is beyond human, who works in the supernatural, on your side. He doesn't want to judge you; he wants to help you. But you have to be honest with yourself and allow him to call out and deal with the things you've been wrestling with.

WATCH FOR SIGNS

Joseph had dreams. Moses saw the burning bush. God gives us signs of what we should be doing. They may not be as dramatic as a talking bush or a pillar of cloud or performing miracles, but we receive signs all of the time.

I had a dream that my music would take me very high, but eventually, I would have to get from behind the organ and use my voice. Now, as I write this book, I can see this starting to come to pass. A sign I ignored was how many people prophesied when

I was younger that I would be a preacher and that someday I'd have books.

Sometimes God uses people to tell us what he's about to do. Historically, these people were prophets—seers and tellers of God's work. But the sign won't always someone telling you his message directly. It may be someone that you meet and help. It may be that someone is profoundly affected by your gift. They might say, "Wow, every time I'm around you, I learn something," or "Every time we talk, it's like you just know what I need to hear to feel better." That's a sign.

God doesn't just use people. You could be thinking heavily on something or pray for the answer to a problem you've been having, and within minutes a song could come on that says exactly what you need to hear. This is something I'm gifted in as a prophetic musician. People come to church not always knowing what they need, but when they hear the music—the sounds, the frequencies, the lyrics—they are opened up for whatever is to come through for them. Maybe you've been in a service like that, where it felt like everything, from the music to the sermon, was speaking straight to you. That's because, in a way, it was. That is a type of sign.

Sometimes, and this is a big one, the sign might be a feeling of uneasiness, as though something is wrong underneath the surface. That is a clue to wait for more clarity. Another sign might be how easy or challenging a path is. If you're trying hard and nothing's working out no matter what you do, that could be a sign that you're in the wrong lane. Slow down, ask for a new sign, and follow it.

TUNE IN

I used the analogy earlier of radio static. Some of you might be familiar with the old-school radios with the tuners on the front.

For those that may be too young to know what that is, the tuner is a dial. Before internet radio and digital stereo systems, when you wanted to change the station on your radio, you had to tune it to the right frequency. You literally had to turn the dial left and right until you hit just the right spot for the sound to come through clearly.

Tuning in to God's voice can be like that. You have to start someone and keep adjusting the dial until you hear the message clearly. In life, this may mean you get a feeling like you're supposed to do something. You can't fully explain it, but it feels right. If you follow it, you find out what happens. Maybe it works out in your favor, better than you expected.

On the other hand, maybe you get that feeling, but logic says it doesn't make sense. Perhaps, like Mahalia Jackson, people around you that it won't work, and you should do something else. Maybe you listen to them instead and end up somewhere you don't want to be.

You'll only know what that "feeling" God gives you is and how it works by trying your best to follow it. Like tuning a radio, you will have to adjust, course correct, and get it wrong a few times until, eventually, you recognize it nine times out of ten. You only get better.

As you fine-tune your vertical alignment, the up-and-down channel, between you and God, you gain access to power and presence that will expand your horizontal, outward reach. You'll have more clarity on your gift and how to use it in your calling to serve your highest purpose. God is the architect of the plan. He already knows the blueprint. If you ask him for the next step, he will show you. You don't have to be afraid to ask. God is fully invested in your success. He trusted you with a gift, gave you a direct plug into his spirit, and said go forth.

As you go out into the world to do your best work, remember who you're plugged into and make sure the connection stays strong. I'll give you one more analogy from modern times. You don't have to rely on wi-fi with God. You have a direct line. Use it. Rely on it as your main source. You'll find your internal "computer" running faster and more stably on this connection.

YOUR GIFT WILL MAKE ROOM FOR YOU

Proverbs 18:16 says, "A man's gift makes room for him and brings him before great men." My gift of music and the heart that God gave me to want to impact services and assist ministers as they're ministering has tagged me as sort of a "preachers musician."

I've been hated for that and talked about for it. Many skilled musicians, some of whom I've looked up to, who play great and have the knowledge and training to do so, have talked about me because they don't understand how I can be on the same platform as them or why these pastors seem to want me so much? It's as if they are asking, "Who are you to be in this arena when you have not been through the things that I've been through to learn to play this instrument." While I don't want to focus on them, I do want to tell you about a time when this gift gave me an unexpected opportunity.

So, there is a major conference in Riverside, California, called the Koinonia conference. They have it every year and invite the biggest mega-pastors in the country and out of the country—T.D. Jakes, your Marvin Sapp, Joel Osteen, Joyce

Meyers, and so many more. Years ago, I received a call from the conference leader for that year. He said, "I need an organ player that not just plays, but flows." A preacher's musician.

I was surprised. They already had some of gospel music's most extraordinary musicians associated with Koinonia. But somehow, my name came up. Andrae Smith, organist and keyboard player from the Inland Empire, who can't read music and has no major connections—or so I thought. You see, God had given me favor with someone that was over the media department who said, "if you are looking for organ player that can play for these preachers, you need to get this guy, Andrae."

At that time, I never would have thought that I would be on an organ playing for anyone of that caliber. But the conference leader heard my friend and they called me.

"Hey, listen," he said, "we don't know if T.D. Jakes is going to bring his organist. We think we know for sure that Marvin Sapp won't have his musician; he wants to have one. Are you willing to come and play for these people for these days?"

I said yes, of course. To be on the same stage as these people was an opportunity I couldn't pass up. I was so elated to be recognized I would have done the job for free and felt honored, but God knew I needed the money that week. What they offered me for the week was unbelievable to me at the time. So, that was one blessing in itself. Then to that put me on a stage that allowed me to play for the likes of Bishop T.D. Jakes and Paul Morton. I actually got to meet his son, Paul Morton Jr., who is a Grammy Award winner now.

Being in Southern California, if they didn't bring their musicians, they could have gone to L.A. got some very top-notch musicians. They could have had whoever that they wanted. But the gift that God gave me to play at extraordinary levels and minister to people through my music placed a brand on me that brought recognition and placed me in the presence of truly great men and women.

It turns out that T.D. Jakes brought his organist. I wouldn't have to play the organ. I still felt blessed and grateful to have been called and even been there with thousands of people at that conference. I was on the stage. I thought my job was done, and I wasn't really needed after all. But then, the organist looks at me and says, "Get on the keyboard."

There was my moment. I thought this would have been a story of how I almost got to play with T.D. Jakes. But God didn't call me there to almost play. He didn't position me to be there "just in case." At that moment, I found myself up there with one of the world's best, and when I got on the keyboard and started playing, T.D. Jakes walked over to me. He stood in front of the keyboard and just started moving—dancing—because his spirit connected. Not with his organist but with my fingers. As I was hitting the keys, his head was moving with it. It was as if he were telling me, showing me, that he was tapped in. He was feeling me, and, in his mind, this kid was anointed.

I tell this story because I want to highlight something called favor. Favor is sometimes defined as approval, support, or a liking for someone. In spiritual terms, there is a concept of divine favor whereby God's purpose for you supersedes what appears to be the natural order of things. I had no "right" to be on that stage or in that conference by my own work and placement in the natural world. I had no badge or credentials proving that I belonged there other than the purpose that God gave me to be there. I could not have worked my way into that space even if I had tried, but the calling on my life gave me unique favor because I could serve a higher purpose.

As I discussed in the previous chapter, when you get into vertical alignment, you become a vessel for so much more than you thought you could be. You accept your position as an embodiment of God's purpose, and you gain access to things that you otherwise would not. I have no way of knowing how many people were moved by that service, but God purposed for me to be there and be a part of something greater than what I had imagined for myself and have all of my needs met just for showing up, saying, "Yes, I'll go."

Like I talked about in Chapter 4, we sometimes have our own agendas or our own visions, and without looking through the lens of intuition, we literally tell God, "No, I'm going to do this my way." When we align ourselves, our desires and actions, with the purpose that we've been called to and act in alignment, the Bible says that all these other things will be added to us. We will receive the desires of our hearts. But first, we must be open. First, we must learn to listen because when we listen, we become useful, and he can tell us where to go and what to do, and we will have the discernment to know what is or isn't going to be good for us.

~

In Chapter 6, I introduced you to David. Now I'd like to tell you a little more about how his anointing lifted him from that shepherd boy to the giant slayer and eventually the king. At a young age, David was a musician (like me). David played the harp. I don't know any history of him being trained to play the harp, but it seems as though it was a gift that God gave him.

There came a time when Saul, the king, was tormented by evil spirits, and he needed a musician. David's gift came up in the conversation of all the good musicians to bring before the king. At that time, David still was just a shepherd, and there were plenty of skilled musicians in Israel. One would think that they would choose someone lauded for their skill in music.

But King Saul needed a musician that was able to understand what he was dealing with spiritually. He needed someone to come and play music that would soothe his spirit and cast those demons from him. David wasn't a musician by trade, but word had gotten around that there was something special in how he played. That set him aside and from all the other musicians. The king's court called for David, and David played. The demons that tormented Saul fled, and Saul made David his musician.

I want to pause here because this is what's at the heart of this chapter. How does a shepherd become the king's musician over all the other trained musicians and music apprentices? Saul wasn't looking for the talent; he needed someone with a higher calling. The scripture says that your gift will make room for you and bring you before great men. David's anointing placed in the presence of the nation's most powerful person. The king was asking for his help. When you use your gift, it will open doors for you and put you into spaces that seem unreal. Remember, there is purpose in all things!

God had already purposed for David to become king in the future years, but what set him up to be king was his gift. The gift put him before the king, which started a relationship that opened doors and eventually made way for him to become king himself.

Another story I love is that of Joseph, the dreamer. Joseph's story is similar to David's; only he went through more trials. It's compelling, and there are many lessons in his story, but for now, we'll just look at his gift and what it did for him. Joseph had a gift of dreaming dreams. He could dream of things that had yet come to pass. More than that, he could interpret the dreams of others. Joseph had a dream that he would be in a position to bring help to his family, in a position of authority, even before his brothers. When he had his dream, he messed up and told his brothers.

You can't always tell everybody your dream. We'll talk more

about this in Chapter 15, but for now, just know that Joseph ended up in a literal and metaphorical pit, which God was able to use toward his higher purpose. Joseph finds himself working as a slave for a great nobleman, Potiphar. Because of the anointing on his life, Joseph rose to the position of master of the house. But there was a bigger purpose still. Joseph's gift was so powerful that Potiphar's wife was attracted to him and wanted to sleep with him. Joseph had enough integrity to say, "No, I'm not about to do that."

Well, as the story goes, Potiphar's wife lied to her husband, and Joseph was thrown in jail (a perfect example of how even when you do the right thing, you may still be tested by those who would seek to harm you). But God had a purpose for that too. In that prison, Joseph interpreted a dream for a man who became a chef in Pharaoh's palace. When the Pharaoh needed someone to interpret a dream that had been plaguing him, the chef told him about Joseph, and, like David, Joseph was called and positioned in a seat of power. Pharaoh gave him his ring and said:

> "Since God has made all this known to you, there is no one so discerning and wise as you... You shall be in charge of my palace, and all my people are to submit to your orders. Only with respect to the throne will I be greater than you... I hereby put you in charge of the whole land of Egypt... I am Pharaoh, but without your word no one will lift hand or foot in all Egypt."
>
> — Genesis 41: 39-44

In this story, the youngest son of a humble family, sold as a slave and kept as a prisoner, ascended to the highest attainable position and made a master in a foreign land. God has purposed for you to prosper and to grow like this. If you are dialed in and aligned, he will turn to you when he needs someone to do a specific job. It won't matter who is involved or what doors need to be opened for you. You will find yourself in the same room as people you may have only looked up to in spaces that you dreamed of (and beyond), and there will be a place for you there.

Before I close this chapter, I want to touch on one more important topic that has to do with purpose and positioning. I mentioned earlier in this book that I had the chance to play for Little Richard and stand-in for Billy Preston, and now I've told you about playing on stage with internationally recognized ministers. These are examples of how God has positioned me because of my gift. But you may be wondering, now, if I'm such a great musician, and I've had these opportunities, why am I not famous? Why am I not touring the world right now? Why am I playing funeral services and local Sunday services? Shouldn't I be elevated to a "higher" position by now like David and Joseph?

There are a couple of answers to these questions. First, there are mistakes, which I'll talk about in Chapter 11. Like David, after becoming king, and even Saul before him, I didn't get everything right. I was blessed to tune in and play, but not every decision I made outside of music aligned with my calling. I had some issues in those days that had not been fully defeated, traumas, bad habits, stubbornness, and even some insecurities. Right when God presents you an opportunity, you know, sometimes the devil shows up and holds your issues in front of your eyes to convince you not to reach for what has already been given to you. I had a certain amount of fear and imposter syndrome because I had not yet learned who I really was.

I doubted that I was as good as these guys in the physical world, not realizing I was just as good or better in the spiritual. And that was why God called me there. This is a mental thing that stops a lot of people from fulfilling their purpose. The Bible says to renew your mind. We have to renew our minds daily because "God has not given us a spirit of fear, but of power, love and a sound mind." A double-minded man is unstable in all his ways, and we need that assurance to show up in our purpose.

The other answer and the one that I want to call your attention to is purpose and affirmation. Neither Joseph nor David had to seek after or pursue their gifts. Neither sought the power and prestige that their callings bestowed. The doors just opened for them. In some situations, you don't have to pursue. I believe the Koinonia conference was an affirming moment for me to know where God wanted me to be in terms of service and the level of anointing that I had. From that, I then needed to understand what my actual calling was. What do I do with this gift? It's not always meant for people to become famous. It's not always meant for people to be rich.

When I was young, I wanted to go on tour. I wanted to do all these things that the famous musicians did. But then, when I realized how people would come to me in different places— walking in a mall or eating at a restaurant, even getting my haircut—they would recognize me. They would say things like, "Are you that organist I saw at such-and-such church? The one who played something like Sesame Street in the middle of a song?" (That was me.) Or like the man who found me in the parking lot to thank me for the song I played for his wife's funeral. My calling isn't about the fame; it's about the impact. I am where God needs me to reach the people in my area right now.

I remember one day I got called to play a gig at a club. I said I couldn't play. I was in service, but I would go and check them out when I got done. They ended up hiring a good friend of mine named Doug. Doug is worldwide. He plays on stages in front of thousands of people and goes out on tour. Now I had never really met Doug in person, so I thought, but when I walked in and Doug saw my face, this man lit up like a kid just seeing his father. I was shocked, and he could probably see it on my face.

"You don't remember me? Do you?" he said.

"No, I don't you don't remember," I said, a little embarrassed.

"Man, I used to come watch you play all the time. Me and this other kid."

As he talked, I started to remember. They were kids, teenagers, and they used to come to a church that I played for. But they used to come on Sunday nights when their mom would let them, just to hear me play the organ and direct the choir. He said what impacted him was that I was able to direct the choir, sing, and play the organ and move all these people. Now both of them are very talented, respected musicians. Doug travels the world, and you can even catch his name attached to some Disney projects. And he just wanted to let me know that I was one of his early inspirations. And So, for me, that affirms I don't have to be famous.

You may be saying to yourself, "I've graduated high school with honors. I went to college and earned my degree. Why am I working at McDonald's? Why am I hustling right now cutting grass? I was so ready to set the world on fire. Why am I not in the corporate arena that I wanted to be in?" You may be wondering how or when God is going to open doors for you.

I just want to remind you, like I had to be reminded, that God has already purposed over your life, these things that you already asked about because he's planned for us to have a good life. He's planned for you to live a fulfilled life. But you must have enough faith to move in ways that can't be explained in the natural. You have to have trust in the invisible hand.

You're not fulfilled in the role you're in for one of two reasons: either your focus is off, and you can't see what's actually happening, or because it is not your best work. If your focus is off, you simply have to look at how God is using you and the moments that are most fulfilling and figure out how to magnify that. If you're not doing your best work, pray for a sign. Ask for guidance on what you're supposed to be doing. Sometimes we get stuck because we're too resistant to surrender to God's plan. But it is the surrender that all of the things can be added. God can fill your cup once you learn to empty it of expectations.

9

USING YOUR GIFT CONFIDENTLY

"For God has not given us a spirit of fear, but of power and of love and of a sound mind."

— 2 TIMOTHY 1:7

Fear. Perhaps the most dangerous four-letter word in English. Fear is the enemy of purpose because if we are too afraid to act on what we know inside, then the knowledge doesn't really matter. We can have god's anointing. We can have God's favor. We can use the scriptures to rebuke the devil and people who are coming against us, but if fear gets inside of our minds. We are still vulnerable. Let me tell you a little bit about fear as referenced in the scripture.

In Chapter 14 of the Book of Matthew, Jesus walks across a lake to meet his disciples in the boat. Now, he was the one who had sent them ahead early. He knew that he would have to walk across uneven water to reach them and that they might be afraid to see him. And they were. In the midst of that storm, they thought he was ghost. So, he called to them saying, "Take courage! It is I. Don't be afraid." (27)

Then Peter said, "Lord if it is you, tell me to come to you on the water." (28)

Jesus called him and Peter stepped from the boat down onto the water, and he began to walk towards Jesus. Imagine being in that moment. There is a storm, the boat you've been on is rocking. The wind is pushing into your face and the waves are splashing you from all directions. Still you see this man on the water and you think, "Well, if he says I can do it, I guess I'll go do it." It takes a lot of courage to get off a boat under normal conditions, but to say, "Yes, Lord. I will come," even though all appearances say you should drown takes more than courage. It takes faith.

By his faith, Peter walked on water. But then, when he realized where he was and how chaotic the scene was, he became afraid and began to sink. (30) You see, even in a moment of faith, when there was clear evidence that he had the power, the favor, the anointing, and God looking right at him, fear crept in and took the miracle from under his feet. And when he saved Peter, Jesus asked, "Why did you doubt?"

Let me tell you one more story. I can remember playing for revival in San Diego back in the day. I was scheduled to play for the service. There was supposed to be singers for praise and worship, but, unfortunately, no one showed up to sing. The pastor that I had traveled there with explained, that because no one was showing up to the praise and worship, I would need to do that.

Oh boy, the first thing I thought was, "Oh, no, not me." I got hat that feeling in my stomach that seemed to tighten and churn and makes your limbs go cold, you know that one you get when you're really nervous about something. Fear had come on suddenly. There was no way I could get out there and sing in front of all those people. That wasn't my thing. They hired me to play. Where was the worship team? There had to be anybody but me.

The pastor convinced me I was going to be alright. So, I went out and sat at my keyboard, looked into the crowd and began to play and sing. I just went right into it, doing my best to hold it together. Well, after a couple of minutes, I could see the spirits of people, and fear came over me again. I got up, just like that, and left the keyboard. I went to the back of the church to talk to the pastor in the office.

"Pastor," I called, "I can't do this. These people are looking at me strange. There are witches in the service."

You know, the pastor thought this was just the funniest thing. He was concerned because I just left the service unattended, and there were people in the congregation looking around wondering what had just happened. Still he laughed and said to me, "You know, we're going to have these type of people that come to the service. That's the type of services that we have. People come to service to be helped. So, you doing praise and worship. Just do what you do because you're going to see the people, but you got to look beyond the people."

That one of the first times where I started to see a gift in me beyond being able to play. It was a prophetic gift, a discerning gift that comes through me, just by opening my mouth and accepting that position as leader. I was not just playing but I had to take this mic and profess. I could see the spirits of the people, and it wasn't really nice. For me, it was downright scary. No one was in there heckling, booing or throwing food at me. It was just the fact that I could see them; I could see into a realm beyond my natural perception. I didn't think I ready.

Pastor laughed again and said, basically, "Listen, you're going to go do this. Hurry up and go get back on the keyboard. If you want to get paid for tonight." He was joking with me, but he knew that if nothing else, I would do it to get paid. That was my personal reason for being there. The honest truth was I needed the money to survive. But me doing God's will helped me in a time of tremendous need, so I was there. That immediately gave me some boldness. Sometimes I imagine God must have been laughing me. A little financial pep talk and the fear was gone real quick.

I said to myself that I was going to get out there and get it done. I convinced myself that I had enough courage to get on that keyboard and go forward with the service, allowing God in. I knew that as soon as I touched that board again, it wouldn't be just me, but God through me. I had to put my faith and focus on God to use me. Now, I could discern what was going on and see past the spirits of the people into the hearts of the people. Those people wouldn't have been in that service if they didn't need some type of help—even if they didn't recognize yet. And that's why I had to be there. Yes, there were some people in the crowd who were considered witches. We call them church witches because they go and sit, because they love the music and the prophecy and things like that. But when it when it comes to really understanding and hearing the Word of God, they don't want to.

So, I had to take that—them staring at me and not blinking and all these things that seemed scary. But it wasn't me. The hearts of these people were not against me. They were against God. It was the god inside of me that they were dealing with at that moment that wanted to get connected to them. And obviously, there was a longing in them too for them even show up in a service. Otherwise, why come? God had a calling on them too. By being willing to show up and be used, I realized that there was a greater purpose at work both for them and for me. God was working on the people, and he was showing me what else he had planted in me.

Had I let fear stop me, I would not have been able to fulfill the purpose God had for me in that service or many services after that. The path to purpose is full of trials like this like this. You'll be asked to take your gift further than you believe is possible. You have to remember that it's not just you, but the God in you working this gift. You have to sew faith to counter fear, and you do that by taking the first steps.

It reminds me of my kids—and they'll probably be embarrassed when they read this. When my son first started to walk, he started with boldness and was walking in 9 months. My daughter had even more confidence and was walking before that. Neither of them as any doubt that they could do it. For most babies, it's a big deal getting over the fear of falling because they are used to crawling. They weren't afraid at all, and to my knowledge they still have that spirit in them twenty-six years later.

Some of us are afraid of falling. We're afraid of trying and failing and losing everything. We're afraid of being embarrassed and laughed at for the rest of our lives. Sometimes we let people get in our ears and trick us into believing we are alone, believing the job is too big. These are all lies. If we can be like these kids and take our steps before that fear sets in, or like Peter when he stepped out on faith, we can accomplish wonders like Moses did in Egypt.

Remember, God did not give you a spirit of fear. You have His spirit. You are his word, living and breathing. If you let him take the lead, you can trust that he will guide you in the right way. He will give you the spiritual armor and tools to do what you have to do. You just have to be willing to show up and say, "Yes. God, I trust you."

10

DEALING WITH DISTRACTIONS

"Let your eyes look directly forward, and your gaze be straight before you. Give careful thought to the paths for your feet and be steadfast in all your ways."

— PROVERBS 4:25-26

I magine this. You pull out your phone to check the time because you need to get your kids from the bus stop at 3:00. You see that the time says 2:30 pm, and you don't have to leave your house for another fifteen minutes. You've got time. You also see your screen is lit up with tiny red bubbles hanging out next to your apps. Notifications. You've got seven unread emails, six messages in Messenger, twenty notifications in the Facebook app, and a pending update in your phone's system settings.

You start checking through the notifications. You clear the emails first because they are usually spam. Then you go to your messages. It's primarily friends commenting on your recent "story." A few "thank yous" clears that up. Next, you open up Facebook. You get ready to open your notifications to see what's there, but before you do, you notice your friend posted a video with about ten laughing emojis. You have to see what's so funny, so you watch it. When it ends, another video starts, and then another.

As you're watching, you get a text message, and the time-stamp says 2:55 pm. 2:55! How did you lose so much time? Whoever it is will have to wait because you need to get to that bus stop now. There's no way you're going to make it before 3:00, though.

What happened? You got distracted. You had enough time to handle your responsibilities until you got side-tracked, and then, suddenly, you did not. I use this example because it's familiar and straightforward, and I'm sure it's happened to some of you reading this book. Maybe it wasn't picking up the kids you got distracted from, but instead, getting out the door to work on time. Or perhaps you've been in a conversation, and somewhere down the line, you realized you had no clue what the other person was talking about because your mind has been some-where else. We've all been there.

Distractions. Along with fear, few things are as destructive to your path of purpose as distractions. In the Bible, they are termed as "temptations." Fortunately, the Bible also says that the temptations we face are common to man and that God will not let us be tempted by anything we can't overcome. Now that you have some clarity around the concepts of purpose and gifting and anointing, I want to talk about distractions because, like fear, they will come up. The devil will use them frequently to try and stop you from fulfilling your purpose.

So, what is a distraction? It is defined in the dictionary as "a thing that directs one's attention away from something else." I don't really like this definition because it's too open, too broad. In the example above, would you say that the text message was a distraction? Sure, it pulled your attention from the videos, but the videos had pulled your attention away from something more important. From now on, I'd like you to think of distractions as a person or object that directs and holds someone's attention away from their intended purpose.

There, now that's clearer and more purposeful. When talking about purpose, we must remember that there is a specific goal or direction that you are moving in. There is a focus. God purposed your life to make a particular impact on the hearts and minds of the people around you. Therefore, a distraction is anything that is designed to pull your attention away from that.

Most people think I'm talking about obstacles here. Yes, obstacles can be distracting. I know how frustrating it is to have a busted tire hours before I need to be at a gig. I know how hard it can be to keep the right mindset when the washer or dryer breaks out of nowhere, and you need to spend time or money that you need trying to fix it. These things have happened to me, and I would consider them obstacles because they stood in the way of me achieving my purpose.

Distractions are a little different. Where an obstacle creates a hard block in the road that says, "you will not go this way," a distraction is more like a sign that says, "Free Ice Cream, this way" and points to a side road you didn't need to take. It's more dangerous because you can recognize an obstacle. It's obviously trying to stop you. A distraction tries to persuade you to stop yourself, and it does this by presenting something you know you want or like.

I'm reminded of another important figure from the Bible, Solomon, son of David and King of Israel. When he became the king, Solomon asked God for wisdom. God made him the wisest king in history, and the kingdom flourished for many years under him. But Solomon had a problem that many of us men can probably relate to. He loved beautiful women, exotic women.

God had warned Israel not to marry women from the pagan nations that surrounded them. He said that they would seduce Israel to infatuations with their gods. Even though he had God's warning, when temptation came, Solomon took it. According to the Bible, he fell in love with these women and kept 700 of them as wives and another 300 concubines. Can you imagine getting caught up 1000 times?! And just like God said, they seduced him into fellowship with their idols and deities, and they distracted him away from his faith with God, who had made him king.

Some people ask, "If Solomon was so wise, how come he couldn't resist?" That's the way that temptations work. It's never something out of the blue. It's always the thing hiding in the back of your mind, which is why we are taught to guard our thoughts. It's the secret desires of our human hearts, which is why we must guard our hearts. Solomon got distracted because he had a mind and spirit fixated on women, and the devil used that against him.

How many men reading this book do you think have been tempted or even distracted by women? Probably all of them. It's not because women are evil. Women are creations of God and are meant for good. A good woman can *save* a man from his own distractions. The Bible says to honor your father *and* your mother. We get distracted because of our own desires. And if you're reading this, as a man, don't think that I'm judging you. I use this example because it is familiar to me.

I can think of many times when I've been playing in the church, the organ or the keyboard, working in God's anointing, and I've gotten distracted. That's right. You can be operating in God's anointing and, in some nebulous way, still have the urges and desires of the flesh. I could see through my spiritual eyes and still notice someone smiling at me with my earthly eyes, even as God was using me at the moment. I remember feeling like I was helping people and hearing from God while at the same time having my eyes on girls and women in the front rows. I remember letting my eyes linger as these girls purposely walked past the organ and thinking, "Oh, she is fine!"

What I saw when I looked through my spiritual eyes, though, was that some of these women had a demonic anointing. Believe it or not, just as God anoints people, Satan anoints people to his purpose. Think about it like this. When Moses went to Pharaoh for the first time, God told him to throw down his rod. When he did, it becomes a serpent. Pharaoh's magicians saw that and said, "Hey, nothing special. We can do that too." Now, of course, God's anointing is more powerful, and it caused Moses' serpent to devour the others. I bring this up because it's important to recognize where someone's anointing is when they approach you.

If I wasn't careful, I could have found myself connected to the spirits of these women and tuning into an anointing that was not of God. Satan will show you what is pleasing to you and make it look right. He'll let you see all the signs and make it look like it's coming from God. He's always wanted to be a duplicate of God. But then he'll throw in something that is meant as a distraction to pull you into his purpose, which is to steal and destroy. He prowls like a lion, seeking someone to destroy. (1 Peter 5:8)

Sometimes Satan knows that he can't reach you directly. He knows your anointing and if you're too strong for him to tempt directly or block with an obstacle. So, what does he do? He finds something you won't recognize as easily. I think about Sampson. God gave him supernatural strength. He was a hero to Israel like Hercules was to the Greeks. If he went to the battle, they were sure to win.

God told Sampson not to cut his hair, and his mother (a good woman) warned him not to tell anyone that his hair was the source of his strength. Remember, when God gives you something, you have to cover it. It's not for everyone to know. Sometimes it's prayer and fasting; sometimes, it's keeping the right

company. There may be some places you can't go or people you
don't give all of your time to because you have to cover what God
has planted in you. Sampson met Delilah, a woman he had no
business with, and she was anointed with a purpose to find his
weakness. She came as a deceiver with a purpose to destroy him,
but because he was distracted, Sampson didn't see the trap. He
told her about his hair, and she cut it off, and he was captured.

I'm not telling you this story to scare you. Sometimes these
messages with so much truth can be shocking and scary, but
again, there is no temptation that is not common to man and
that God doesn't already understand. There is nothing to tempt
you that you cannot overcome. You just have to know how to see
it. See it and cover yourself.

You may be reading this book as someone who knows they
are anointed. You may be a young preacher, a fifteen-year-old
young man or woman, and you know that God's called you. You
may feel peer pressure from your friends to do things that aren't
good for you, like smoking, drinking, staying out light, being
sexually involved with people you barely know. But you don't do
these things because you're different. You may even be made fun
of because you walk and talk like a preacher at fifteen when
everyone else does the things that fifteen-year-olds do. Do know,
there's a cover. Cover that anointing, even if your friends or your
household doesn't understand. Sometimes God uses people who
aren't our families to show us the way and help us to understand
our callings.

Don't feel bad if you are who God made you to be. Trust,
there is a reason you can't, and you don't feel comfortable in
some positions and settings. It's that inner anointing saying it
wants to be covered. It doesn't feel good in that position. Know
that. Those things will save you from being in places where
young people have been shot for being at the wrong place at the
wrong time. Playing for so many funerals, I've seen so much

young life lost because a bullet meant for one person ended up hitting them instead. If you've got good parents, mind them. God uses your parents to be responsible for you. They may keep you from specific spaces based on a feeling or a parental intuition. There's a covering there.

No matter your age or where you are in your journey, just remember to stay vigilant. Some situations or people are not what they say or seem. It is up to you to discern whether a situation or a person is pulling you away from your purpose. It may not even be intentional on their part. The thing is, everyone has their own role for you based on their stories and their needs. You have to live the one that God gives you. You can't get caught up living for others and then try to live for God. You can live for God and show up in spaces where you are recognized, appreciated, and supported, where people will have your back and provide cover for your gift when you need it.

11

MAKING MISTAKES

Mistakes. I've made a few... too many to mention here. I believe that someone here reading the book feels like they have made so many mistakes. They may have been told they have made so many mistakes that they can't come back from them. They may have been told they are a mistake and that they would never be anything. You may be in this position now, wondering how you can get back on track.

The first thing I want to tell you is that you are not alone. Everyone makes mistakes sometimes. In my life, I've made many mistakes, and God has had to come and rescue me because no one else could. For instance, when I was young, I got enticed to try to make some money. A situation came about where I could go across the border to Tijuana and bring back a certain amount of illegal drugs. If successful, I would get paid. Now, I am not a drug dealer. I don't know a thing about selling drugs. What the devil had planned was to get me really caught up because I wasn't just selling drugs on the corner. I was going to be transporting it from one country to the next., something that, if caught, could take me out and lock me up for fifteen to twenty years, easy.

It wasn't a complicated job. Someone else might have been able to get away with it. The minute I went, though, the very first time I tried to go down there and do it, I got caught. Busted. I didn't know what to do. I had never been in a situation like that to know to ask for a lawyer or anything. I just became terrified and went with what they were saying and doing.

"Yeah, so you've got a boat full of fifty (I think it was fifty) kilos of cocaine," said the agent who had come in to talk to me. "You'll be going to jail for at least twenty-five years. There's a good chance you won't see your family again for a long time. You got kids, Andrae?"

"Yes. I got kids," I said. The agent could probably see me sweating and shaking in my chair. "I got a son and a daughter. Man, I want to see my kids, sir. That wasn't cocaine on that boat. It was supposed to just be marijuana."

That was my next big mistake. These agents were smart, and they knew what they were doing the whole time. They knew what was in the boat.

The man said, "Yes. Thank you. Now you've just confirmed that you knew what was in the boat. So, you can't come back and say you didn't know. We have you on tape saying you knew what was in there."

I was so "shook." What was I going to do? I was caught. They got a confession out of me without even trying. The man left the room and came back with a file. He opened it on the table in front of me and told me to look. In this folder were documents, records with my name on them. When and where I was born. Who my parents were. Who my wife and kids were. There were also pictures. To this day, I have no idea how they obtained these, but there were pictures of me playing the organ at different churches. All he had to say was, "Is this you?" Of course, I said yes. I was going to jail anyway; lying wasn't going to help me.

he told me he already knew everything he needed to know about me. He knew. I wasn't behind this, and that I wasn't a criminal. (Thank God.) he wasn't really even interested in me. What he wanted was for me to testify. You see, I wasn't alone on this trip. I had brought a friend along who might be able to help and who I knew could have used some of the money. These federal agents wanted me to testify against him because of what they had on him. I called him out of his purpose and into this situation, and they were making him the scapegoat.

Isn't it something how, when you step out of the cover of your anointing, the devil will use you to disrupt someone else too? Not only was he after me, but he was also after my friend, who I had brought into this mess. These agents were preparing to put everything on him. And I felt bad. Again, I was responsible here. I had made a mistake, and I was the one who invited this young man into this situation. But there I was. I either put everything on this friend like the man said, or the devil got us both. There was no real way out of this one. We could not save ourselves.

Fortunately, God still had a purpose and plan for both of us. My friend and I got two different paths. God purposed for me to get out of this situation with nothing but probation and an order to go to therapy. He wanted me to get my act together and stay off that path so I could get back to his work. His purpose for my friend was to sit there and understand who he (God) was, to see for himself that God was going to deliver him out of this—even though it wasn't his fault. Yes, you can say he was still responsible because he made a choice to ride with me. That would be fair, and God would have had to deal with his heart on that. Either way, the two of us were wrapped up in one big mistake that God was going to use to reveal himself.

God said, basically, "Look, I'm not going to let this bad situation take you out." I got probation with therapy to deal with myself. My friend had to stay in jail through his trial, but he got acquitted. Even though I had to testify against him, and the agents made this whole case against him, he was acquitted and let go. I can only think that God was giving him whatever time that he needed for God to break through and become real for my friend.

Besides not trying to cross the border with illegal drugs, one major lesson I took from this was that even when we make mistakes, God is still there. He was there the whole time, and he called us out of the situation we put ourselves in. On top of that, he used it as an opportunity to grow both of us so that the next time, we would have more faith and more wisdom to walk the covered path.

Another important point when talking about mistakes is having an awareness of and remembering who you are in God. When we make mistakes, we can be like Adam and Eve in the garden of Eden. We feel guilty and want to hide from God, from our shame. This is because we are identifying with the guilt and letting that define who we are. We are allowing ourselves to be called by guilt and by shame and by depression when really God has already called us by other names. He's said we are blessed, anointed, loved, forgiven.

God already knows that we are going to mess up, and he loves us and stands by us. He will cover us as long as we turn to him and have that transparency, I mentioned in Chapter 7. He knows our hearts and can work with us if we answer to his name. Too many times, we let ourselves be called out of our character, out of who we are, and we become bound by those qualities in our minds.

Before she passed, my mom told me that when it comes to relationships, never be with somebody that changes who I am or my character. At the time, I was going through a rough relationship, a toxic relationship. My partner and I would fight, and she would bring up all of the things that I ever did "to her." She would call up all the ways that I had wronged her and then label me. She named me cruel. She named me heartless. She named me womanizer. She named me the villain. And over time, as we continued seeing each other, I began to adopt those characteristics. She would speak these things over me so much that she would draw them out of me. But it was because I responded to the labels that I became bound to them, and they changed me.

You know who you are. People will speak their visions and intentions over you, but that is not you. You are what God says you are. Sometimes you act out of character, but that doesn't make you unworthy. Back in the day, when children misbehaved, parents would say, "Quit acting up" and "Why are you acting out?" This is because Parents knew how they raised their children, who they really were. They knew that the behaviors were not them. This is how God deals with us. God could have let my friend and me go to jail for those drugs, but he wanted his children back. He wanted us to know, "This is now who you are. I made you better than this." And he set us each on the right path, according to his purpose.

Also, keep in mind that your history will never limit what God has in store for your future. You may have a lifetime of mistakes stacked against you. God doesn't look at your record; he looks at your purpose and your willingness. He knew you before he called you and all the things you had done. He wants you anyway. Just like how I can play in clerical and secular arenas, God needs you because your trials make you someone who can reach the hearts of others who may be lost in depression, fear, confusion, and darkness.

The Bible has an entire cast of imperfect people from many different backgrounds, many of whom were not saints before they were called. In the New Testament, Saul, also called Paul, was known for persecuting Christians before the Holy Spirit appeared to him. Zacchaeus was a tax collector and called a sinner, but Jesus stayed in his house. Moses had a temper and had killed a man in Egypt. Your past does not define you. Once you decide to answer your calling, your history becomes irrelevant. You are who God calls you to be.

Remember this: mistakes will come. People will tell you you're doing the wrong thing. Some people will try to catch you up and trap you in them to bind you. Sometimes, people will tell you that you are a mistake, that you don't deserve to be on that stage or in that job or at that school, or even that you weren't supposed to be born. Know this: there are no mistakes in God. When we think that we make a mistake, God steps in and turns pain, struggle, strife, and ruin into purpose. You are purpose.

12

WHEN GOD PUTS HIS FINGER ON YOU

D o you remember my friend from the previous chapter? The one who had to spend time in jail after getting roped into my mistakes? Like I told you, his trial ended with him being wholly acquitted, and he was set free. If you're like me, you have thought the question, "If God was going to deliver him anyway, why let him spend so much time in jail?"

If you're in the Church, you may be smiling because you think you know the answer. Obviously, God wanted to reveal himself and bring glory to his name. By leaving my friend in jail, God would have made it clear that he was the one that got him out. Right? Like Peter being freed by the Angel, right?

Or maybe God was testing him? He wanted to see what was really in my friend's heart. Would my friend have faith while in the "fiery furnace" like Shadrach, Meshach, and Abednego or like Daniel in the lion's den? This testimony would definitely convince people that God is real.

What if I told you there could have been another purpose? Remember our working understanding of purpose, which is to sway the hearts of men toward God. Sometimes God needs a way to deal with people's hearts that is free from distraction. Sometimes he needs to get us into a space, spiritually and physically, where the only thing we can do is look up at him. We can't go left or right because there's nothing there but wall. There are no cell phone notifications to take away our attention. It's just us. And in that space, God's voice, the still small voice that lives inside us, can finally minister to the heart and start cleaning things up inside.

Sometimes, God has to put his finger on us to get us into that space, where we have nothing to do but be still and look up. Have you ever used your hand to hold a piece of paper in place? It's like that; only God doesn't want to use his whole hand. One finger is heavy enough to keep us pinned for as long as he needs to while he's dealing with our hearts.

Imagine for a moment how my friend and I ended up in that situation. We both needed money. We both saw an opportunity. We both knew it was wrong, but we tried to do it anyway. Why? At least for me, the situation had become so desperate that this seemed like the easy way out. I had already made a fair share of mistakes and been around people who were no spiritual good for me. I was stubborn, and even though I knew where God was pulling me, I thought I would do things my way.

Have you ever been in a situation like that? Where you see some signs or have an idea of what you're supposed to do but insist on making your own plan? (As if we can "out-plan" God) You wouldn't be the first. Jonah ran from God and chose the path of disobedience. He was called to spread God's message of salvation to the people of Nineveh, but he thought that God was wrong and chose to go as far from that assignment as possible. God had to cause so much trouble for Jonah that Jonah finally repented and went back to his purpose.

What neither Jonah, my friend, nor I realized was that we were not only acting rebelliously, but we were catching ourselves up in our own traps. Like stepping into quicksand and insisting that we could swim out. Struggling only makes it worse! We were in quicksand, and God needed us to be still. For me, God only needed a wake-up call. I can only imagine what my friend must have been going through for God to need to bring such a hard stop to all activity. He must have been sinking faster than I was.

If you think about it, that is a covering. Like I talked about in the last chapter, God is in the midst with us. He will let us stumble like a watchful parent, but he won't let us fall. And like a good parent, if we stubbornly throw ourselves into trouble, again and again, he will put a stop to it by holding us down, temporarily. For our own good, he puts his finger on us so that we are not lost. That is what the enemy wants, for use to get lost.

The devil knows what's in our minds and will tempt us. He will deceive us and seduce us away from our purpose until we can no longer see the truth from the lies. Like a spider, he spins webs and waits for us to get stuck. Then he strikes with attacks like depression, poor health, anger, and suicide. Tragedy is waiting for us if we are not careful, but God is watchful and knows what is out there. He doesn't let us stray too far or wander for too long. He puts his finger on us and says, "Be still and wait on me. My child, you were on the road to ruin, and now it is time for you to see. I've got you. Cast your cares on me, and I will be your strength and provide everything you need."

It's not a punishment; it is a covering. It is a reminder that you are branded, and you are his. It's a reminder that he cares and is ever-present. He puts his finger on you when you're too close to a boundary that he doesn't want you to cross.

Another reason God may put his finger on you is that he knows you're not ready to advance. This may show up in a few different ways. For instance, there may be a promotion at your job, and you keep getting passed over. You may be trying to buy a house somewhere, but every place you look at gets bought before you can make an offer. You may be looking for a new relationship, but it's as though there's no one around.

This doesn't necessarily mean your desires are wrong. As I said in a previous chapter, your focus might be a little off. However, it could just be that God is trying to prepare you. He's putting you through what T.D. Jakes calls resistance training. If you go to the gym regularly, you know what he's talking about. There are free weights and treadmills, and machines of all kinds at the gym. The devices work through resistance. You don't have to add more weight to intensify the workout; you increase the resistance, forcing your muscles to work harder and get stronger over time. As an athlete, you go through resistance training to build the strength you'll need for competition. In life, you go through resistance training to build strength for the journey ahead or perfect a skill.

For instance, you may be called to be a preacher. You have the gift of confidence and of words, and people listen when you speak; however, you have a weakness for studying. You get distracted easily and don't get into the books like you need to. In ministry, you must study. You'll have to know the word of God and when and how to use it. You'll have to know how to deliver it in a way that people can understand, which means you need a deeper understanding than the average person. If you don't study, how will you deepen your knowledge?

You may say, "God tells me what to say. I hear his voice, and I listen." That's all well and good, but God also tells us to study the scriptures. If we don't, how can we know God's word and will from Satan, who will appear in a form that may look like God to you? If you don't study, you won't be ready to take up your calling in ministry. You would put the congregation at risk, and God can't let that happen.

I think about how the Hebrews had to wander in the desert for 40 years until the faithless generation had died off. This is often taught as a punishment. Because they were disobedient, they could not enter the promised land. I invite you to get a little more practical with God's thinking. The promised land was already inhabited by other people. God was going to deliver it to them, but he needed a generation of people who understood faith and obedience, who would not look at obstacles and blame God for their troubles and challenges. So, he made Israel wait and wait and wait until they were ready to take his next steps and follow what he says.

I've mentioned readiness a few times in this book so far. But, in the context of waiting and training, I want to dig a little deeper into what it means. I heard a message from Pastor Marvin Sapp while playing for him at the Koinonia conference. He said he was buying jewelry once, and he was just curious to know when the person who extracts the gold knows that the gold is ready? How can they tell that it's the best that it can be and ready to be made into the lavish jewelry that we buy?

So, he asked his jeweler, and the jeweler said, "Well, that's an interesting question. The process is simple. You have to put a lot of heat into the gold for it to reach the point where you're able to use it. As it heats, the dirt, minerals, and impurities rise to the surface, and the goldsmith skims it off. The goldsmith knows he's done when he can see his reflection in the gold like he's looking in a mirror."

There is no recipe or set time. The goldsmith doesn't crank up the heat for forty-five minutes, and then it's done. No, he has to keep a close eye on it. He has to work on it and continue this skimming or refining process until he can literally see himself in the product. The work is done when his image shines clearly, but until then, the gold stays in the heat so he can keep working.

The message here was that sometimes we will feel like we are in intense heat (or under intense pressure), and we are just stuck there. Sometimes, we get real uncomfortable where we are, but it's like we just can't move and nothing we try seems to be working out. This is because we are like the gold, and God is the smith. He is holding us to that heat until we are ready, until he can see himself in us.

And so, God is like that, in our lives. He sees us as gold. We are his treasure. We are his purpose. He's going to keep working on us until we are shining and pure because that's when he knows we will reflect him to the people. That's when he knows that we can handle what is coming and still shine. We will go through the fire, and sometimes we'll feel like God is gone. But he's not. He's skimming us, purifying us, using the fire to do his work in us so we can do his work in the world.

∼

You may be somewhere right now that feels too hot to handle. You might feel like your life has been stalled, and you can't move forward. You may be wondering how to tell whether God has his finger on you or if you're in a test. In those moments, pray and meditate. I'll be honest. It is hard to know the difference at times because it can look and feel the same. But there are some signs you can watch out for.

You can tell when you're going through a trial or facing opposition because you will have some victories. It may be small or slow, but you will see them ramping up. You are simply going through it and the only thing you can do is ask God for the strength to Endure. It's like when Jesus went into the wilderness to fast before the crucifixion. He knew what was coming and prayed that the Father would take that cup from him. He was going through real torment and real fear. But then he gave up his will and prayed, "Not my will, but Thy will be done." He remembered who was carrying him even through the trial.

When God's asking you to be still, that feels very different.

You will feel like none of the things you want to do are available to you. There are no victories. You will find yourself struggling in vain until there is nothing else around, and you have to ask, "What do I do now?" This was Jonah in the belly of the big fish. He had nowhere left to go. He had reached that spiritual rock bottom, and he knew it. Likewise, you will probably recognize, at that point, that you've been acting up. The moment you do, the path forward becomes clearer. There will only be one, and it is the one that points you to God's purpose for you.

Check in with your spiritual practice and make sure your channel is clear. Make sure that you're listening to God. He may be asking you to endure, or he may be asking you to be still. It becomes easier to discern the more you can listen and respond rather than guess.

13

FORGIVENESS

Over the last few chapters, we've spent a considerable amount of time talking about pitfalls. You know, distractions, mistakes, and being held up so we can grow. We talked about getting so uncomfortable that it feels like we are being destroyed when God is actually refining us. We talked about what the journey can look and feel like when you've made mistakes and need to get back on course. In this chapter, I would like to spend just a little time talking about how to start taking those next steps forward. It begins with forgiveness.

For the Christian, Forgiveness is major. It is the foundation of our faith and the only thing we can stand on. Forgiveness is a type of anointing that allows us to remain in God's favor even when we act out. If it weren't for forgiveness that God continues to show, we would not have hope. You can't get around it, go under it, or climb over it. You have to deal with things and receive.

If you're reading this book, you most likely completely understand how forgiveness applies to our faith. Now I want to talk a little about how it applies to your purpose, specifically your journey. You see, guilt and shame are paralyzing forces. They cause people to hide from God and avoid their callings because they don't want to face the sense of condemnation. Instead, these people play small and lie low. Or worse yet, they give themselves over to the ways of the world because they believe that they have messed up too badly. You must not think this way about yourself. Doing so is like allowing another name than what God has called you to take root and define you.

Do you remember how I told you that David made mistakes? He slept with a married woman and had her husband killed. He was a villain at that moment, not a hero. But would you believe me if I told you that God forgave him? While David's house did fall into trouble, God still called him "A man after [his] own heart." David's anointing as the king still stood, and for his sake, God had mercy on Solomon and Israel.

Zacchaeus, the tax collector who climbed the sycamore. He was forgiven. Jesus said, "Salvation has come to this house today" because Zacchaeus answered and confessed when he was called. He was transparent with himself and God and took the opportunity at a second chance.

What I'm getting at here, and hopefully it is clear to you now, is that God has a purpose for you that can't get turned off because of a few mistakes. If you are willing to confess what you have done and come before God honestly, you'll be forgiven. According to some teachings, you are already forgiven. That is where some people struggle. They never learned how to receive forgiveness. A parent or guardian was too hard on them, and they became hard on themselves. They hear, "You are already forgiven," but their minds still tell them, "You are not worthy." They have not learned to see God as a redeemer, and because of that, they become bound by their mistakes.

If you are to move forward in your path to purpose, you must understand forgiveness. Like connection, I'm going to say that it moves in two directions. First is vertical, and that is your alignment with God. You get right with him first, and he forgives you. The second is lateral. You forgive yourself and others. The flow of forgiveness is the manifestation of God's purpose. He didn't come to condemn the world but to save it. We are his working arms and legs, the living epistles representing this truth. To fulfill this purpose, we must embody forgiveness.

VERTICAL

When Jesus hung on the cross, nails in his hands and feet, blood leaking from a wound in his side where he was stabbed, a crown of thorns pressed into his head, he prayed. He said, "Father forgive them, for they know not what they do." This is the compassion he has. Even those who have turned on him can be forgiven. This is so hugely important to remember because this is the first connection to God that Satan will try to destroy.

Remember, Satan is the accuser. If you know you've done wrong and been guilty, he will use that against you. The devil is called the Father of Lies, but the Bible doesn't necessarily say that he will lie to you about what you've done. You know what you've done, and he'll use that against you. The truth may be that you are guilty of the very thing he said you did. The lie he twists in is that you will always be guilty and that you are irredeemable.

His whole goal is to make you feel so guilty that you feel there is no hope. He wants you to succumb to depression. He wants to destroy your peace to the point where you become spiritually dead. You may not have any physical problems at first, but once you spiritually die—or just become spiritually ill—you can start to develop physical breakdowns and unexplained health conditions. This is because your mind is not at peace, and your mind controls what your body experiences and does. Doctors today have confirmed the physical damage that too much stress can cause on the human body. Imagine living in that.

But listen. God is the redeemer. God says, "I've got you. I've got your sorrow. I've got what you've done. I will forgive it, and I will forgive you. I will remember it no more." The Bible says that God delights in mercy and will throw our iniquities into the sea of forgetfulness. Can you picture how vast that sea must be? I remember looking out at the ocean as a kid in awe that it had no end. That is how far away God will throw your faults if you are in him and willing to come to him and trust in his word and in his plan.

The Bible says God is the righteous judge. He does shun wickedness. He does judge us. But he doesn't judge us by our shortcomings. He doesn't judge us by how we act sometimes. He judges us by who we are, and he looks at us through his Son, Jesus. Jesus already conquered judgment for us. For the believer, this means Satan can accuse you, but the accusations are already recorded, taken to trial, and dealt with on your behalf. All you have to do is believe in him, be honest about what you've done and make the conscious effort to be better. To leave as much of the past in the past as you can and look to God to do what you can't.

HORIZONTAL

Knowing that the only one who can judge you has already forgiven you is powerful. This means two things: (1) You can forgive yourself. You can follow God's example and let your mistakes be what they are, mistakes. You don't have to define yourself by them or spend your life searching for repentance or hiding from judgement. The truth can and does set you free. (2) You have an example of how to deal with others.

God delights in mercy and favors those who are humble and

forgive. If he, the supreme, has forgiven humankind, are we not to be like him and forgive others? Are we above God to where we can judge each other? No!

People will do you wrong. They will hate on you, talk about you, call you out of your character, and even lead you into trouble. Forgive them. Forgive, and show kindness. First of all, judgment is not your job. Your job is to heal and be a benefit of others. Remember? To whom much is given, much is required. Jonah was a prophet who chose to judge when God had decided to forgive. Jonah thought he was above God and became angry when God chose mercy. This is an example of how not to behave. Neither your calling nor your faith makes you capable of judging the hearts of men and women.

This is where some Church folks go wrong. We sometimes call them the "perfect saints," and they are the equivalent of the Pharisees in the Bible. These are the holier-than-thou types. They think they are closer to God because they know the scripture and live parts of the word—waking up speaking in tongues and casting blessings and curses instead of saying a simple "good morning." And these are the type of people that turn folks away from the church.

People who need God most (we all need him, but some are hurting) need to feel God's love and be inspired by his grace. They need to be healed and brought into the family of Christ. These perfect saints make the church look judgmental and don't belong, or like these people have to give up being normal and only talk about the Bible all day. Ultimately, they end up doing some of the devil's work for him.

Knowing that we are all forgiveness and receive vertically, our job is to extend that grace outward. We are the fishers of men that Jesus mentions. Our nets are love and forgiveness. Our bait is our gifts.

~

There are many things that you can take away from this book, but if nothing else, remember this! Forgiveness is at the heart of everything you do. It is compassion in action. If you are called to a higher purpose—no matter what purpose, assignment, or mission you are called to or what gift you have, forgiveness is what saves people from tragedy. This includes us.

Many great people, talented, gifted, anointed people get stuck in lives that don't fill their cups. I've seen men and women drink themselves into an early grave, even because they haven't forgiven themselves for mistakes that were made. Sometimes, the things consuming them weren't even their fault, but grief and shame overtook them. Now that you recognize this, I hope you can take it with you and be kind to yourself and others.

14

JEALOUSY IS THE ENEMY OF PURPOSE

Being a musician, I've seen many bands form and then fall apart over the years. The obligation to show up to rehearsals and play at the gigs often conflicts with some of the musicians' personal schedules, especially if they have families and regular jobs. For those of us who make music our livelihood, it is essential to find people who can be relied on.

Another reason that some bands fall apart is that the sounds don't always blend the way they should. When you bring people together who are used to playing in certain styles or who have never played in a band before, you sometimes have friction, and the music doesn't create the atmosphere that it needs to. When this happens, a musician may occasionally get their check for the night and not get called back.

One of the most common breakdowns I see, though, is jealousy. One person in the band may have gotten more spotlight and attention than someone else. Someone may get more solos, more shout outs or more tips at the end of the night, and what is supposed to be different artists coming together to create a unique sound, you get competition within the band. All of this because someone is jealous of the attention that someone else gets.

Now, this sort of thing doesn't just happen in the music industry. It can creep into any and every corner of our lives. In relationships, one partner might become jealous and suspicious of the time the other is spending with certain friends. At work, you might find yourself bothered by the amount of praise your peer gets when you work just as hard. In the church, one clergy member may become envious of the favor that another one has with the pastor.

I can recall times when I was called to play and then later asked to lead praise and worship even though the church ad a minister of music or a choir director. This was the result of my gift, the anointing that God gave me. It wasn't that I was trying to steal the show or take anyone's job or role within their church. After I got older and learned to flow and pay attention to the ministry over my ego, I would show up to services to play and find myself asked to take, and sometimes outright given without much choice, the leadership role within that church. The anointing gave me favor where my gift was needed over someone's knowledge or experience.

As I said in Chapter 8, this sometimes caused the people around me, even those I considered friends, to stop talking to me or start talking about me. And I can understand why. Who was I to take their place? I was just the organist. I must have done something behind closed doors to get in with the pastor like that. In reality, I just had favor at those specific times, and much to some people's disappointment, favor isn't fair. Sometimes, it will give you opportunities you haven't earned and have no claim to other than that God gave them to you. But if God gave it, your lack of experience or work doesn't make it any less yours. God knows the plans he has for you.

I think about David. He was a shepherd who God anointed to

be the next king of Israel. What right did he have? he had no lineage, nor was he one of King Saul's descendants. He was the one Saul called as a servant to play music at night. When Saul realized God's anointing over David, he was enraged and filled with envy. He tried to kill David.

Envy also appears in the New Testament. The Pharisees and priesthood of the day took major issue with Jesus until, finally, they could have him arrested. In the book of Mark Chapter 15, it says, speaking of Pilate at the trial of Jesus, "For he knew that the chief priests had delivered him for envy." Pilate, a Roman governor, a conqueror over Israel, saw that he had done no wrong and that the priests—the church people—were just jealous of the praise he was receiving. The ones that should have had Jesus' back were the ones that became so consumed by jealousy that they had him put to death.

Hopefully, you're starting to see the theme here. You're going to have people that become jealous. Even if you're not proclaiming that you follow Jesus, the spirit of jealousy will be there. Satan was Jealous of God. Right? If you're trying to do good and you have a gift, life will bring you some jealousy, especially when you decide to come out of bad situations—when you transform your life when you should have been destroyed. (Isn't it interesting how some people can literally root for you your failure and destruction like they placed a bet on you?) These people are like Jonah, hungry to see their vision of justice because they have their own opinions of how the world should work.

But where does that type of anger and negativity come from, to begin with? What makes people so hell-bent on watching others struggle? (And some people don't care if you're doing well or not until they see you doing better than they are.) For one, these people have too much ego. Their pride makes them believe that they should be receiving praise, glory, and opportunity.

Their pride makes them seek attention and spotlight even when they don't need it. You can get recognized for your work, and because you were recognized, their pride tells them that they should be noticed too.

The second reason is comparison. Listen. You can't get jealous if you mind your own business. If you're focused on what you're supposed to be doing instead of watching everyone else, you don't have time or attention to spend being jealous. You wouldn't even know what someone else got to become jealous of in the first place. Jealousy is a thief of joy, and therefore an enemy of purpose because it disrupts your peace and distracts you from your calling.

GUARD AGAINST JEALOUSY OUTSIDE

Sometimes the closest people to you are the ones who do the most damage. For example, you might go through something with someone only to find out that they aren't cool with you anymore once you get out of it. These people are miserable and don't want you to outgrow them or your need for them. This could be for many reasons, from not wanting to be alone to not wanting to feel like a failure next to you.

That's how comparison works. They aren't looking at your success as proof of what they could do. Jealous see your success as you leaving them behind. You're abandoning them. You're pretending to be better than them. You're getting something that you don't deserve, and it's not fair. In their minds, your success reflects all the things they could be but are unwilling to be or unsuccessful at so far.

Envy comes from a sense of pain and a feeling of worthless-ness. Of course, if you tell a person this, they'll say, "Me? Jealous of you?" and proceed to list all of the things they have going for them. The problem is that they don't believe what they're saying.

In their minds, they still feel like they're not enough. In their hearts, they're wishing they had the favor, blessing, or anointing that you have.

These people need love. These people need compassion. These people need reassurance that God is on their side too. Be an encourager and pray for them too. For you to be in your purpose, you must be able to extend forgiveness to them.

Then, there are successful people who may or may not know you but hate the idea of anyone, especially someone with no name or claim to their stage, taking up space in their niche. In all of their comparisons, they fail to realize that there is no competition in God's plan. Everyone has their place, and if they were in theirs, they would have no reason for them to be jealous of you.

These people need your prayers, not your attention. God will deal with them in his way, but he needs you to stay in your lane. The plan was not yours, so their opposition is not directed at you. This means the fight is not yours. Let God handle it.

But remain vigilant. These people will try to speak things over you and lay traps for you, like Daniel before he was thrown into the lion's den. The king's men were jealous and conspired against him. They made it illegal for Daniel to remain obedient to God. Because Daniel stayed in his purpose, they were able to capture him. But remember, they could not harm him. The spirit of God closed the lion's mouth and caused the king to feel regret.

GUARD AGAINST JEALOUSY WITHIN

Jealousy is not only a problem you will face from the outside. You will have to deal with it inside of yourself too. Being anointed does not make you immune to human challenges. You may find yourself struggling in some periods of your life while others flourish. You may be in a season of stillness while God has his finger on you, and yet others with similar gifts or callings are having the success you wanted.

In my career, I've mentored a lot of young musicians in one way or another. Sometimes directly teaching them and helping them to develop their ear. Sometimes as more of an inspiration. It is always a double-edged sword seeing them get major gigs and start getting invited to tour. On the one hand, I am grateful to have impacted their path and set them on a course. But, on the other hand, how dare they take what I've taught them and go out further than me!

Of course, I'm joking in that last line, but you see, I'm writing this book, and I am not immune to jealousy. It's going to happen from time to time, and the best way I've found to deal with it is to remind myself of who I am. I use words of affirmation of my gift.

God said that the power of life and death are in the tongue. So you should speak words of affirmation and faith over yourself daily. I am somebody. I am blessed. I am the head and not the tail. I am the lender and not the borrower. I am blessed; I'm blessing the city; I'm blessing the field. I'm blessed when I come and when I go. These are the lines from the word of God that I speak over my life. As I speak them, they cancel out the negative things that other people, Satan, and my mind may say to me. I don't have to be jealous if God says I'm all these things.

BE GRATEFUL FOR YOUR TREASURES

Have you ever met someone who just seems like they can do it all? You know the type of person I'm talking about here. The ones with multiple college degrees and who have run companies. The ones who manage to get up and go to the gym when the rest of us are sleeping and then still have the energy to get through the day. The ones who can sing, play multiple instruments, speak well (maybe even in more than one language, and captivate people all without breaking a sweat.

They show up, and all of a sudden, your confidence just deflates because you know that for every good thing you've achieved, they've got at least five stories just like it. It's easy to look at those people and be jealous. From the outside, they have it all. They have multiple gifts, and they are proficient in using them. But remember, the grass is not always greener on the other side.

There is no use being jealous of these people. You have no idea what all they or their family has had to go through to be able to bear that level of anointing. You have no idea what trials they've had to endure or what kind of pressure they may be under even now. Remember to whom much is given, much is required. A person can have multiple gifts and anointings. But for each one, there is another level of responsibility added to that person's plate. That's not to suggest that with each new reward comes a new burden. I'm just saying that you can't assume that their life is any better than yours or that just because they can do all these things, you are also gifted in ways that they could not imagine.

I'm always amazed at the child prodigies who can play an instrument and get good at it and then keep picking up new instruments like it's nothing. So it is no surprise when they get accepted to world-renowned music institutions and learn to read, compose, and direct music at the highest levels. I've seen a few of these individuals and thought they were insanely talented. Sometimes I've even been intimidated by how gifted they are. But when they see me play, having all the gifts they have, these people still look up to me and wonder how I do what I do. That just goes to show that no two people's anointings are the same. And that makes sense because no two people have the same calling, story, or qualities.

We have to be thankful for the gift that we do have. Each gift is a treasure designed and giving with purpose in mind as a perfect fit for the person to whom it was given. Each of us has at least one gift that no one else has. Even if the talent is the same on the surface, it is defined by what you bring to it and how God intends to use you. That makes you unique, and for that, you can practice gratitude every day.

15

HUMILITY & RESPONSIBILITY

One lesson I always remember when it comes to humility comes from my mom and dad. Back when I first started playing for services, they noticed how the people in the church people had a way of building me up. You know how sometimes people will put you on this pedestal when they see a gift in you? Well, my mom and dad used to say, "Always remember, when somebody praises you, you give that praise back to God. You didn't go through lessons or training. You're a miracle." When someone praises me as Andrae, it's easy for me to want to take that. But that's what Lucifer did. He took the praise. He took the credit. So, I always try give the praises back to God because he made me. He made my gift.

Another thing that my parents used to say was, "Remember, there's always somebody out there better than you. There's a big world." As good as God had blessed me to be, there were other he could use. As I got older, I started The Nam show, which is one of the world's biggest music conventions. I started seeing those four- and five-year-old kids that can play circles around what I've been playing for last thirty years. There's always somebody out there better. I was called, and yes, I was irreplaceable as a person, but God could unseat me in my calling like he had with Saul.

What people don't realize is that your character has a lot to do with how God uses you. You must maintain your vertical alignment with God in your spirit. Not just with your gift. Not just with your mission. Otherwise, it's like one of my pastor's used to say, "Your gift or your calling can take you places that your character can't keep you."

Think about that. Your gift and calling can take you places that your character can't keep you. If you have character flaws and make mistakes, you will be forgiven, but you can miss, and mess up opportunities that God lined up for you. He really wanted me to understand that my gifts, or my calling my gift to play can put me in some really good places, but if I let my bad habits and flaws remain consistent, I could mess up the calling on my life.

For instance, I used to get called to play at a few big churches. Everybody loved me because of the way I played. I was good, and I could flow. However, I have a character flaw. I was perpetually late. Service would start at 7:00 am, and I would show up at 7:00 or even 7:15. On time would have been to show up at 6:30 so that I could prepare. But at the time, I knew the service didn't really start until I started playing, so I didn't really take it seriously. These pastors wanted me for a time. But some places aren't like that. Some places wouldn't call back.

I have a good friend named Dave. Because of my gift, he opened an opportunity for me to play in Palm Springs amongst, millionaires and billionaires. This is a space where, if it weren't for me gift and my connection to Dave, I really wouldn't be allowed in. My gift allowed me to be able to come there and be respected. But my character flaw of not taking the time seriously and handling my business like I should have got me caught up.

In this instance, I actually just misunderstood the time. When I got the gig, I was told that the time was 7:00, this was the "downtime." Now, I wasn't entirely clear on that, but I didn't ask what they meant by the downtime. What time did they want me there? I had to learn a lesson about communication and clarity here. I thought downtime meant for us to show up there to start unloading and getting prepared. His use of the word "downtime" meant the time that the show started. I didn't show up at 7, though. I figured with 7:00 downtime, the show would be at 8:00, and I got there at 7:45. When I arrived, the band was already finishing their first set. I had completely missed the first 45 minutes of the show.

The band didn't make a scene. The band leader on the guitar, one of the multi-millionaires at this club, just looked at me and said to get set up. Oh! And he was sure to tell me, "You're full of sh**, Andrae."

This is where humility and integrity come into play. I had legitimately made a mistake. I didn't intend on being late. But when he said that, I had to own it because it was still up to me to make sure that I got clarity. Not only that but had I arrived at 7:00 like they had said, it would not have been so bad. Instead, I had habit of running late that I let get in the way here. I messed up. I could have been angry or rude. I could have gotten proud and told him off, but I would have been wrong. I needed to swallow my pride, own up to my mistake and apologize. So, he said I was full of crap. And we left it that way. I started to play on the next part of the gig.

The first Keyboard solo came up, and he gave it to me. I started ripping that piano up. I was going to a make up for me being late and let them know that my presence was there. We were doing good. I was feeling better, and the band was vibing. Then at a point in the song, he adlibbed the lyrics which said, "Come on now! Don't be late," to "Come on, Andrae. Don't be late!" That was his way of, you know, kind of calling me out me in front of all these millionaires. It was like he was saying, "Thanks for that big old solo that you just gave us just a minute ago. But next time, don't be late dude." But that moral of the story, here, is that there was no next time. As much as I love Dave, even to this day. I have not been called back to go back up there and play since that day over six years ago.

Dave and I laugh about it now, and I may have even thanked him once because he taught me something important about responsibility. As I have said numerous times in this book, to whom much is given, much is required. Where I messed up was that I didn't respect my responsibility with my gift. God opened a door for me that I wasn't ready to honor. He let me see with my own eyes, the consequences of letting my character flaws get the better of me.

I consider myself a man of God and call myself blessed. When we say these things, we are making ourselves representatives of him. We show God in all that we do and to whoever we are in front of. No matter what we're doing, people see us and think, "This is what God looks like in people." What good would it do if God allowed me to show up in that space again and be late again? People would think that God and Christians, have low integrity. We don't respect time or honor commitments. That is not a good look.

Because I know who I am in Christ, I know that I am forgiven and that I am still loved, blessed, anointed, and useful. But in this instance, I messed up a blessing God had for me and missed a chance to bless some others. Go placed someone else who is more reliable in that space. As you seek to move forward in your purpose, it is important to remember that wearing your badge means you have a responsibility to uphold the charge you've been given. You have to show yourself and the One you represent in the best light possible at all times.

You don't have to be perfect. We won't be, and God knows it. But you must be accountable. You must be sincere. You must make every effort to do the right thing so that when you make a mistake, it is not a blemish on your reputation. You must be humble enough to admit when you make a mistake so that it doesn't become a character flaw but a teachable moment. If you are humble, you are still useful. God opposed the proud and exalts the humble.

16

YOU ARE MORE THAN YOUR CALLING

You are not what you do. You are more than your calling. Knowing the difference between your work (even in service to God) and your identity to maintain a balanced and healthy life is essential. Yes, you have a gift. Yes, you have been called. Yes, you have a big responsibility (to whom much is— well, I won't say it again). However, you cannot let these things consume all of your thoughts. You do still have to live in the world and take care of yourself. You have your family who needs your time and attention. You have to make time for your health and well-being. You need to allot time for fun, for sleep, and for meditation.

The statement "you are more than you're calling" reminds me of a statement that I would hear growing up from certain pastors. They would say that sometimes people are so heavenly-minded that they are no earthly good. You can be so deep into the things of God that if I come and say, "Hello," you can't say, "Hello" back. Instead, you start speaking in tongues. You can be so "drunk" on the Spirit, that you take no pleasure in daily life, and it can show in how you interact with people.

I can remember one pastor I knew who wanted me to meet his wife. He had just gotten married, and she was the first lady of his church. He was so excited for me to meet her, and he told me all these great things about her. She was strong in God. She was a prophetess. She was devoted to her faith. I was excited to meet her too.

When he introduced us, he said, "Honey, this is Andrae. He's a powerful keyboard player." I smiled and reached my hand out to shake hers. To my surprise, she never really addressed me; she just put her hand out and kept walking. No eye-contact. No sincerity. No actual acknowledgment that I was there. But when she put her hand out, it was as if to say I was not worthy enough to shake your hand. I admit that it offended me some because I was going to play for this woman afterward.

Jesus was not like that, you know, Jesus, out of all people, could have been the one to say, "Hey, I'm the Son of God. Put some respect on my name." Instead, he got out with the people and fellowshipped. He never compromised his character or his position. But if the people were there, and they went to him saying they needed wine, he would pray and provide for them, whether it was food enough to feed 5000 people or just some wine for the celebration. Jesus dined with the so-called sinners, and the Pharisees asked, how is it that Jesus can, can eat and sit and fellowship with them? What does light have with darkness?

Jesus understood he was still living on earth and having an Earth-bound experience. He knew that having the Spirit of God doesn't mean you can't enjoy some things of life and the world. There are times to celebrate and be merry. There are times to experience sexual pleasure (within marriage). There are times to joke. God has planned all of this. And Jesus understood that he could partake so long as he maintained his standards. The people were able to enjoy his presence. Those who weren't believers could experience him being a human and get to know and love him as a representation of God. He could infiltrate spaces where the chief priests were not welcome.

This is a major point that I want to talk about briefly. In the church, there are a lot of people that need help. The clergy is supposed to be ministering to them and helping them. The church is supposed to be a place of healing, redemption, fellowship, and the presence of God. And yet, people are not attracted to the church. Jesus said, "Go ye therefore into the world and preach and teach and bring people to church," but we can't seem to bring people to church. Why? Well, one reason there is a lot of "show" in the church. You have to look a certain way. You have to talk a certain way. You have to be cleansed of your impurities so that you can relate to people. We welcome people without letting them know that it's a place for them.

One more reason is the gift or anointing—or rather our mentality with this gift. We can be so heavenly-minded that if a person walked off the street into our church, they wouldn't know what's happening, and they wouldn't get a clear, simple solution to their problem. They would get a whole lot of "church talk." They would get all the glamor and pageantry. Or they'd get berated with scripture or asked all these questions about their past. Suddenly it feels like they're on trial. When what they may need at the time is for someone to say, "What's your name? Come sit with me. I'll introduce you to our family. I'm glad you're here." They may need to hear the pastor say, "You're going through it now, but there is hope. You don't have to carry guilt forever."

Kirk Franklin has a song called "I Smile." It's all about smiling through the struggle, keeping your eyes on the future God has planned, and knowing that it's going to be okay. I think that's the whole reason why Jesus came in the first place—not to condemn, but to lift people out of the darkness. That was his purpose, his reason, his calling. So, he had to be presentable and approachable. When we talk about and understanding who you are, and not just your calling, remember that you a human being, a person.

Getting back to the point of this discussion, sometimes we get so wrapped up in trying to follow our callings that we miss the purpose. Sometimes we forget just to be genuine and honest. To be kind. To fellowship and be a friend. You're not here to save everyone, but by just being a good steward on this planet, by keeping a humble spirit, by making a conscious effort to do more good than harm, you can point them to the one who can save them and lift them up.

LIVE YOUR HUMAN LIFE

Allowing yourself to be human means recognizing your human needs for things like food, water, exercise, sleep, fun, and silence. It means acknowledging that you have human responsibilities. You can't get so busy out there working your gift and calling that your family at home is deserted. You can't be so caught up that you have no time to take your children to the park or have dinner with your parents or clean your own house. You are expected to maintain balance in all spheres of your life.

Sometimes this balance takes time to learn because there are hurdles to overcome. It may require you to seek counseling from a professional or even just someone you look up to or another minister. I know you may be focused right now, focused and working hard all the time to take care of your family. But let me ask you this: if you're working all the time, when do you get to spend quality time with them? Do you know that your kids are going through some things at school? Do you know your mom has a major surgery coming up that she's been afraid to tell you about? Do you know that your wife is feeling lonely in your marriage?

You may be chasing down your passion, trying to live your purpose and rise to the level that you think you should be at, but you can't sacrifice what matters most to you to get there. You have to remember your WHY. What is the reason that you do what you do? How much is it worth to you? You may be tempted to say it's for your family, but also ask yourself, is this true? In what ways do your present actions support and strengthen your family? In what ways have you let them down? If they are your why, in what ways can you show up better with them and not just for them?

We have to be able to connect with people. Connecting with people is not always easy. A lot of gifted people, especially musicians, tend to seclude ourselves. Artists and writers are the same way. It's like we put ourselves into this bubble. It's a "nobody understands me" bubble or an "I've got to do this thing now" bubble. When you get in your bubbles, you don't allow the ones who need to come in, the ones who have a place and purpose in your life to help you or for you to be a help to them, to have a natural relationship with you. Man is not an island unto himself. We thrive on the relationships we build together.

RENEW YOUR MIND

The Bible talks about renewing our minds daily. This means to check in with yourself and to take time out of your day for rest and silence—prayer and meditation. This may be as short as five minutes or as long as an hour, but you need that time to foster your connection with God and with yourself. Often when we commit to a life of service and purpose, we neglect our needs. We say we're not tired when we are. We say we're not hurting when we are.

You must always be able to self-examine. You cannot stay busy all the time for mental, physical, or spiritual health. For a lot of church people, this may also mean honoring the Sabbath on Saturday or Sunday. That is your time to recollect on your week or attend a service and allow yourself to be ministered to. You may hear something that connects with your personal life now that you would miss if you stayed so intent on doing the work.

We must check on ourselves, just like we have to check the tires on our cars. If you don't check those tires and just ride, you may keep going until something happens. I've had these happenings a few times. I've had to get a ride to church because my tire was flat. And when the technicians looked at my tire, they told me the tire was shot anyway, and I was lucky not to be on the freeway. If I had paid attention to my tires, I wouldn't have had that flat tire. I would have paid a little money for a new one and been alright. Instead, I had to buy a new tire and pay for a tow truck too. Now, every so often, I check my tires, the coolant level, check the oil level, and such so I can spot issues or take preventative measures.

Are you taking preventative measures in your life? Self-care is how we do that. Do you have time to spend with loved ones? Do you have time to invest in your own happiness? If you like documentaries and superhero movies like I do, do you ever take time to watch them? Do you have a gym membership that you're not using? It is spiritual to live your human life.

HANG UP YOUR CAPE

Sometimes you need to become unavailable or go incognito. Think about your favorite hero if you have one. They have their powers and their gifts, but many of them are not superheroes 100% of the time. Batman is Bruce Wayne, who runs a company. When he's needed, he puts his suit on, and then he's Batman. Superman has his powers consistently, but he doesn't live in those powers all the time. He is Clark Kent, and he has a job. He tries to fit in with the world. When it's time for him to save the world, then he pulls his shirt open and reveals that 'S' on his chest. He saves the day, and when he's done, he goes back incognito.

There's a lesson in that too. He says, "You know, I just want to be that guy that's just reporting things. I don't want everybody to know who I am. I want to save the world, but I don't need the spotlight." There's a certain level of humility in that, and with humility comes more power and elevation. God exalts the humble and increases their lives.

There is more to you than the cape and the powers—or in our real-world case, our suits and anointings. There is a real person underneath all of that who needs to receive love, compassion, peace, solitude, joy, and prosperity. There is a real person with emotions and desires. If you are to continue walking your purpose, you must avoid burning yourself out, which happens when you do not make time to take care of yourself.

17

LOOKING AHEAD

W ell, here we are. We have reached the end of this book, this journey we set out on sixteen chapters ago. You should now have at least some idea of what purpose, gifts and callings are and how to start to recognize yours. Before I send you back into the world to answer your calling and start walking in your purpose, I feel compelled to share a few more messages with you.

YOU'RE ON A JOURNEY

Life is a journey. Another word for a journey is a "voyage," and voyages are long, sometimes challenging quests. I think of the old Star Trek series. I was never a huge fan, but I remember they were always out in space exploring planets with other creatures. I don't recall them ever coming back to Earth. They were on a journey to discover the universe (to my understanding, at least), and this journey took them to uncharted, unexpected places. I can only imagine being on one of those ships. With each new trial, you learn a little bit and get a little more experience.

That's how life is. When you're on a journey, it implies a certain amount of discovery, meaning you won't know all the things that will come up for you. You won't know the right thing to do every time. Sometimes there will be hardships, and you'll feel like you're under a lot of pressure. Sometimes it will be like driving in fog, and all you can do is hope and pray that you don't crash.

What I want you to remember is that all of this is normal. It is the journey. If things get difficult, it could be a sign that you've veered off the path. It could just as easily mean that you have come so close to fulfilling some aspect of your purpose that the devil will try anything and everything to stop you. You may have unexpected financial trouble or unusual tension in your marriage or a string of bad luck that doesn't seem to let up. The only way to know what is going on is to strengthen the channel between you and God so that you can hear him. Focus on him and let him guide you.

The Bible teaches us to cast our cares upon the Lord and that he will sustain us. This means we do not have to be consumed by worry, anxiety, stress, and fear. We can trust his plan supersedes what is immediately in front of us and that all things are being worked out for our highest good. We will come out stronger, wiser, and better than before, more equipped for the rest of the journey. And I say "we" here because I am still on my journey. My walk isn't done.

IT TAKES COURAGE

It takes a lot of bravery to go boldly towards your purpose, even when the world would tell you otherwise. Go anyway. I knew at a young age that I just wanted to play music. There was a passion there that I wanted to make my living with. It wasn't always easy, and some would say my life might have been easier had I finished school and found a regular job. But that was not my calling.

I had to have the courage to stand firm in what I believed my purpose to be. I had to trust the gift I was given, and the doors that were opening were signs that I was on the right path. I had to have the internal confidence to believe that God would have my back. He put me on the path; of course he would provide for me! Matthew 6 says:

> "Look at the birds in the air. They don't plant or harvest or store food in barns. But your heavenly Father feeds the birds. And you know that you are worth much more than the birds. You cannot add any time to your life by worrying about it. And why do you worry about clothes? Look at the flowers in the field. See how they grow. They don't work or make clothes for themselves."

If you are going to walk your purpose, you must have courageous faith, the kind that makes you believe that if God says it, you can walk on water and heal the sick and cast out evil. That is the spirit in each of us. If God gave you the gift and the assignment, then you've been branded, and you will have his favor.

ALWAYS STAY HUMBLE

When God calls you to your purpose, you may be blessed with extraordinary talent and favor. That's not for you to go and exalt yourself. Lucifer was the most beautiful angel in Heaven, but his pride was his undoing. He thought he could be equal to God and set himself up to oppose God. For this, he lost his favor, his anointing, and his place.

There is an obvious lesson here for us. Our gifts are not our own, but God's to give and use. They are given with purpose, and to whom much is given, much is required. We are expected to benefit others. The only way to benefit others is to be of service and to be in alignment. The only way to be genuinely aligned and have the heart to serve is to be humble.

When I played at my first solo funeral and put the woman in the ambulance, I was not humble. I was trying to have a show. I wanted the attention on me. I should have taken a backseat and tapped into the spirit so that I could give to these people who were already hurting. When you are proud, you cannot hear and therefore cannot serve your highest good. Be confident in your place, but always remember that you have a place because of the anointing which comes from God.

You should have so much confidence, which comes from truly knowing who you are and the God in you, that you can be humble without feeling belittled. Beware of becoming so spiritual that you are no earthly good. Jesus didn't condemn people; he fellowshipped and healed. If we are his disciples, we must follow that example. He already showed us the way. If you're too proud to have a heart-to-heart conversation with someone because they live differently than you, how can you help them? How can your gift reach them? You aren't tuned into the spirit. You're in your ego.

Take pride in your gift, but don't get yourself caught up with delusions of grandeur.

For those of you reading this book who have made it this far, I can only assume you've made it this far because you are ready to go on this journey. You are prepared for a drastic shift in your life. I want you to know that if you feel it, that longing, that tug on your heart to do more and be more, your instincts are correct. It is time.

I told the story, previously, of Jesus and the Samaritan woman at the well. After she left to tell the townspeople to "come see this man," Jesus' disciples returned. He tells them that the fields are already ripe and ready for harvest. In his metaphor, the fields are towns full of people waiting to be turned to God. He is telling them that the hour is here, and those who are working are already receiving their rewards.

I'm not implying that you have a calling in ministry. Your calling could be anything, just like your gift. What I am saying, though, is that your purpose affects more than just you, and out there somewhere, someone is waiting for what you have to offer. Someone is outside your gate waiting for crumbs. Will you share with them? Someone is on a bus stop, crying for a miracle. Will you be the answer to that prayer?

As I close the pages of this book, I have one more thing to tell you. It is never too late to start living your purpose. You've never made too many mistakes. You cannot be too far lost to make a difference in someone else's life. You may go through hardship. In fact, that's almost guaranteed. Joseph, David, Daniel, Moses, Job (especially Job)—all of them had to go through trials. Things happened that weren't their fault. Things happened that were their fault. But God was still able to use them and their stories for the greater purpose. If you allow yourself to be used, you can uncover a new meaning behind your life story.

You may have childhood trauma. You may have health issues. You may have marital problems. You may not be in your children's lives. You may be working in fast food or retail because you didn't finish high school. None of this makes you any less worthy. If you are humble, courageous, and willing to go on the journey, then your mess can become your message. Your pain can become your purpose. You can live the life and build the legacy you were destined to have. Start now.

ACKNOWLEDGEMENTS

While I wish I could name and thank all the people who've impacted my life and helped me to become who I am now, I simply do not have the space because there are so many of you. Just know that I haven't forgotten you!

For now, I want to share my gratitude to some of the people who have contributed to this book coming to light. From my son, who showed me it was possible and daughters who believed in me, to the close friends in my life who have assured me it was time. To my band mates, who's have shown up for me in ways that remind me that God is good and will always have a plan for me.

I want to acknowledge the men and women of God who have prayed with and for me and who have prophesied over me. I've said before that sometimes it is not our works, faith or favor that covers us but the prayers and intercessions of those who love us. Thank you to those who have blessed me in this way. Without you I couldn't have become the person to deliver this message.

Last, but certainly not least, I want to give thanks and glory to God, who has been my father, the good shepherd, my rock and my sustenance during this journey. He promised never to leave nor forsake me, and I can say that even when I felt lost, he always knew right where I was and kept me from the hands of those whose purpose was to destroy me.

You all have my sincerest gratitude.

ABOUT THE AUTHOR

Andrae Smith is a prominent organist, keyboard player and producer in Southern California. Named after gospel music legend, Andrae Crouch, Andrae was raised in the Church where his musical journey began at around age thirteen. His mom—a talented singer, herself—prayed that he would play music, and almost immediately his ears were opened to the power of music.

Over the last thirty years, Andrae's passion for music has opened many doors in his career, from playing the organ and directing choirs for church services across Southern California to becoming one of the most respected and sought after organists and keyboard players in his region and in multiple genres. As a live musician, he has performed across the country and shared the stage with such prominent artists as Rev. Al Sharpton, Marvin Sapp, Billy Preston and the legendary Little Richard, to name a few.

Andrae believes in the power that music has to move crowds and is known to take songs in unexpected directions as guided by the Spirit to take his listeners on a journey. This, he believes, is a part of his unique gift and how he can walk in his purpose. It was through this path that he has come to realize a calling toward ministry on his life. Although others in high positions have prophesied that he would do great works beyond sharing his music, it was not until he began thinking seriously about this book that Andrae began to believe it.

Many people hear the call, but don't answer it right away, don't believe it is for them, convince themselves that they are meant to be one thing. What Andrae wants to share now is his understanding that we were meant for more—that the plan for our lives is greater than we can see from where we are, but if we can walk in faith, we can have more confidence, more joy, and more fulfillment than we imagined was possible.

THANK YOU

Once again, I'd like to thank you for reading my book and trusting me with a part of your journey. Walking in your purpose isn't always easy. Sometimes, like me and many others, you will stumble and take what seems like the wrong turn, but if you keep going, you will find that you are being covered and guided all the while.

My prayer for you, now, is that you find your way and remember how to keep finding it every time you feel lost. I pray that you are blessed with all that you have been promised and that you open your heart to receive it. Finally, I pray that this book moves you, stirs you to take whatever steps you need to get into alignment with your purpose.

We are all walking our paths and doing our best to learn, every day. I'm no different. For anyone who would like to join me on this journey, you can follow me on my social media pages below. I know I'll be seeing you soon!

—Andrae

Facebook: https://www.facebook.com/andrae.smith.50

Instagram: @smith.andrae

CPSIA information can be obtained
at www.ICGtesting.com
Printed in the USA
LVHW091338300621
691571LV00001B/37